Logical Investing

The Fluff, The Bark

& The Bite

By Edward Moldaver

Second Edition

Enigami & Rednow Publishers, New York.

Copyright 2016 by Edward Moldaver.

All rights reserved. Printed in the United States of America. Excerpt as permitted under the United States Copyright Act of 1976.No part of this publication may be reproduced or distributed in any form or by any means, or stored in a database or retrieval system, without the prior written permission of the publisher.The views, opinions and ideas expressed in this book are solely those of the author, Edward Moldaver. They are not necessarily those of any organization, corporation, entity or person with whom the author presently has, in the past has had, or may in the future have, a business connection, including Barclays and any of its affiliates, and Stifel the acquirer of Barclays US Wealth Operations.

This publication is designed to provide accurate and authoritative information in regard to the subject matter covered. All information in the book is the property of Edward Moldaver or the information providers and is protected by copyright and intellectual property laws. You may not reproduce, retransmit, disseminate, sell, publish, broadcast, or circulate the information or material in this book without the express written consent of Edward Moldaver or the other information providers herein. This book does not constitute investment advice from Edward Moldaver, his publisher, affiliates, Barclays, or any other organization to which Edward Moldaver was, is currently or will be affiliated.

This book contains statements and statistics that have been obtained from sources believed to be reliable but are not guaranteed as to accuracy or completeness. Neither Mr. Moldaver nor the information providers can guarantee the accuracy, completeness, or timeliness of the information in this book, including, but not limited to, information originating with Edward Moldaver, or licensed by Edward Moldaver, or from information providers, or gathered by Edward Moldaver or from publicly available sources. There may be omissions or inaccuracies in the information contained in this book, neither Mr. Moldaver, the publisher, nor any information providers shall have any liability, contingent or otherwise, for the accuracy, completeness, or timeliness of the information, or for any decision made, or action taken by you in reliance on the information in this book. Neither Mr. Moldaver, the publisher nor the information providers make any representations about the suitability of the information contained in the book and all such information is provided "as is" without warranty of any kind.

Library of Congress Cataloging – in – publication data

ISBN NO: 978-0997322392 | Enigami & Rednow Publishers, New York.

Logical Investing: Bringing Certainty in Uncertain Times/by Edward Moldaver – First Edition.

Praise for Edward Moldaver and for "Logical Investing"

Larry Kudlow--Host, CNBC's "The Kudlow Report"

"I can see there is a very good reason that Barron's named you as a number one financial advisor."

Ron Kruszewski--CEO of Stifel Financial

"In Logical Investing, a must-read for serious investors, Ed shines a new light on investing by distilling it down to its most basic concepts, calling upon the often overlooked values of common sense, tangible evidence, and personal experience."

Barron's – "America's Top Financial Advisors"

The #1 Financial Advisor in the State of New Jersey

The Honorable David A. Paterson--The Governor who balanced the New York State budget.

"Ed is a super advisor whose clients collectively paid many millions of dollars for him to represent their interests in the market. As one of them, it was worth every penny."

Alan "Ace" Greenberg--Chairman of Bear Stearns from 1978 to 1993, Author of "Memos from the Chairman"

"Ed Moldaver is one of the guys that make this country great! He came over in 1978 from Russia and has become a major contributor in helping this country remain great."

Dedications

With great respect:

To my team at The Moldaver Group - the greatest examples of excellence in financial planning I have ever known.

The Moldaver Team

With great love:

To my most important team - my wonderful wife Eve and my children, Jenna, Danny and Nick.

My Most Important Team--My Beautiful Family

Acknowledgments

There are several people and organizations without which this book could never have become a reality.

I first wish to acknowledge New York Jets Ring of Honor Inductee and certainly the MVP on our team, Wayne Chrebet, of The Moldaver Group, also known as The Moldaver, Lee and Chrebet Group, who is anyone's idea of a great teammate for his insatiable quest for success on and off the football field.

I also want to acknowledge the other Members of The Moldaver Group: James J. (Jimmy) Lee, Mary Sliwa, Michael A. von Borsig and Mary Bennett, who followed me and maintained continuity for all our clients as I moved to ever more client-centric organizations. Onward and upward to you all! I especially thank Mary Sliwa, a constant inspiration to me in the conception and completion of this book.

I'd like to welcome and acknowledge the newest member of our team, Governor David Paterson. When he took office, he was charged with one the hardest financial tasks anywhere, balancing the $140 Billion New York State budget. He did a complete and remarkable job. After that, any financial task is easy for him.

And I would like to thank my mentor Alan "Ace" Greenberg, Chairman of Bear Stearns from 1978 to 1993, and author of "Memos from the Chairman" for his instruction on building an ACE team.

I also thank Adriane Berg, CEO of Generation Bold Consulting, experts in reaching the boomer investor, for identifying the logic of my investment style from which the organization of this book followed.

I would like to acknowledge John Bowden, CEO of CEG Worldwide, a terrific coach to financial professionals everywhere, for providing the model by which I do business.

With special thanks to my writing guru and daughter, Jenna, for her work as line editor and proofreader. Without her assistance, this book would never be as compelling and articulate as it is today.

Finally, I would like to thank my wife, Eve, and our children, Jenna, Danny and Nick, to whom I dedicate this book. I also acknowledge the immense love and compassion of my parents, Sam and Inna Moldaver, who immigrated to the United States from Russia to give me the opportunity to find my calling. I thank them for the freedom of spirit to love what I do and do what I love with honesty and integrity, and for helping me understand that love and logic are compatible.

Table of Contents

Preface by James P. O'Shaughnessy

Part I: The Illogic Epidemic

Chapter 1. A Simple Doggy Analogy That Can Save Your Future

Chapter 2. The Bark and The Bite of Financial History

Chapter 3. How The Fluff and the Bark Affect Your Psyche

Chapter 4. The Bite of Dispassion

Chapter 5. The Bite of Knowledge

Chapter 6. The Bite of Experience

Part II: There is an "I" in Bite and an "I" in Team

Chapter 7. Building a Wealth Management Infrastructure with Bite

Chapter 8. The Great Big Bite: Behavioral Finance, How to Match Your Temperament with Your Decisions

Chapter 9. Longevity and Behavioral Finance

Chapter 10. Financial Assumptions and How We Create an Infrastructure for Decision Making

Chapter 11. How Are You with Risk?

Chapter 12. Know What You Are Worth

Part III: Fluff, Bark, Bite, Bite, Bite

Chapter 13. Beware of the Gray Brochure - The Fluff

Chapter 14. Just The Bite

Chapter 15. The Relationship of Asset Allocations to Your Goals

Chapter 16. Finding the Rate of Return of an Investment

Chapter 17. How to Pick a Rate of Return That Is Right for You

Chapter 18. Asset Allocation to Improve The Bite

Part IV: Entrepreneurs Need Bite

Chapter 19. Everyone Barks at the Entrepreneur

Chapter 20. The Four Problems of Successful Entrepreneurs

Chapter 21. Before the Parade Passes By

Part V: Financial Life Management

Chapter 22. The Art of Advanced Planning

Chapter 23. A Word about Tax Planning

Chapter 24. To Your Health

Chapter 25. Gifts and Trusts

Part VI: Coming to a Logical Conclusion

Chapter 26. Creating a Logical Path with Bite

Appendix I: The Oracle at Delphi Says: "Know Thyself"

Appendix II: Trust Terminology

Appendix III: Logic - A Very Short Course

Appendix IV: What Billionaires Know

Preface

By James P. O'Shaughnessy

Over 16 years ago, I wrote: "What Works on Wall Street." The title alludes to the best performing investment strategies that improve your results when you can overcome your emotional reactions in the short-term and stay with one of these proven methods for success over the long term.

In every edition of my book since then, I focused not only on what works on Wall Street but also who works on Wall Street. Today, in the aftermath of "too big to fail," bailouts and a recession that cost millions their jobs, the issue of who your advisor is may be of deeper importance than which individual stock or mutual fund you buy.

Time and again, we learn the hard lesson that planning works, and that shooting from the hip, following the herd and being influenced by the latest trend does not. Yet, as with any discipline, staying with a focused investment program is difficult without a coach, advisor and/or team leader.

Now, in his book, *Logical Investing,* Ed Moldaver explains how the right financial advisor/money manager operates to keep your portfolio humming in good times and bad. When Ed speaks, it is surely worth listening, as he has been named the number one financial advisor in the State of New Jersey by Barron's in 2012. This is no small feat, as there are at least twenty-five thousand others in the competition.

But, are accolades enough for you as a business owner, family leader and investor, to put your faith and trust in an advisor?

Although both Ed and I have done well in being recognized for our work, we think not. It is important that you understand what makes your advisors tick and what they are willing to do to create a team dedicated to your financial health. Just as there are winning investment strategies, there are winning decision-making strategies and processes of management.

Few financial books, and we all know they proliferate almost as much as diet books, delve into the issues of how to stick with your strategy in down markets, how to create a communication process with your advisors even if they have discretionary management over your portfolio, and how to integrate risk and personal goals so that your investments mature when you need money the most. Like me, Ed is keen on not only behavioral finance, bringing a plethora of expertise in taxation, estate planning and health planning into the equation, but also the psychology of investing.

The essence of Ed's system, and clearly what he thinks "works on Wall Street," is Logic: a commodity hard to come by in these uncertain times. How does one infuse logic into an investment portfolio? To paraphrase another famous book: so that we can reduce the "random" nature of our walk down Wall Street.

The logical answer comes in several steps that you will enjoy following as you read Ed's book. More than once in its pages, you will be asked to tell your financial and familial story, to probe your risk tolerance, to articulate and clarify your goals. Your participation in these interactive questions is essential in reaping the benefits of this book.

Logic begins with "know thyself," as one of the questionnaires in the Appendix advises you, calling forth the Oracle at Delphi.

But, self-understanding can be no more than a booby prize if you do not also know the next steps to fulfill your goals. That takes investment know-how.

Ed guides you every step of the way with investment performance strategies and analytics that bring logical certainty to tough investment decisions.

Finally, comes the hardest part in the quest for investment logic: staying with your formula and not deviating. This takes active management and discipline. The four horsemen of the investment apocalypse, Fear, Greed, Hope and Ignorance, are the daily fodder feeding our uncertainty in these economic times. Not only does Ed's book help reduce the uncertainty many have about successful investing, it also shows how to conquer the fear, greed, hope and ignorance that destroy most investors' results.

This brings me to an important part of your results from investments.

Do you like travel, learning, business, family, adventure? What is your passion?

What might such questions have to do with investment results?

Quite a bit, actually. The purpose of investing, for most of us, is much more than simply the bottom line. For most, the investment is a means to an end - retirement, college for the kids, lifelong travel and philanthropy. Money must be functional, and so planning is more than getting to a number. It is also having that secure number available to us when we need money to fulfill our goals. The aspect of financial planning that takes into consideration timing, taxes and goals is often called "advanced planning."

In the demographic environment in which we currently live, there is an additional aspect: "longevity planning." This takes into account the health care costs of chronic care, the cost of college when we are older parents, the caregiving expenses for our parents and life fulfillment in our post-retirement years, which can surpass 30 years.

Ed knows that you will need as much guidance on these life issues as on the investment decisions you must make to carry out your goals, family and business responsibilities.

But, whether our concerns are current or future financial security, we are privileged to live in a time when computers can forecast and analyze our portfolio performance and give us some certainty in uncertain times. Nothing could be more logical than using an objective computer calculation to determine whether your portfolio choices adhere to the method you have adopted as most in keeping with your goals and risk tolerance.

In the pages of this book, Ed introduces you to programs

designed just for such analysis. I hope the information will convince you that taking charge and not randomizing your investment decisions will make a true difference in your financial peace of mind.

And so I come full circle. There are methods that work on Wall Street and then there are people who work on Wall Street. I am quite pleased that you have an opportunity to encounter both in the logical pages you are about to read.

Part I: The Illogic Epidemic

Chapter 1

A Simple Doggy Analogy That Can Save Your Future

You might be surprised that the difference between the so-called 1% and the 99% might be more a matter of who advises them, than what they know on their own.

In good times, people feel certain about the markets. It is just that some people think things will certainly be good forever, and others think things will certainly be bad pretty soon!

They tend to act illogically either way.

Later on in Chapter 9, you will read about behavioral finance for a better understanding of why we stay illogical even when circumstances change.

But knowing the reasons for illogical behavior, in and of itself, will not make your bottom line grow any faster.

A wise woman once told me, "Understanding why is the Holy Grail." I want to help you do something about your illogical ways so you make the right financial decisions, and understand why you make errors.

One of those important financial decisions is who to choose and who to avoid when it comes to your advisor.

Let us start with how I came up with the subtitle for this book, *The Fluff, The Bark & The Bite*.

I see plenty of illogical financial moves, most being made by professional advisors. How do they get chosen? How do they get away with losses and still keep clients?

Some of the attraction is Fluff: a high-class office, a great brochure. If it looks good, it must be good. Some of the attraction is Bark: prestigious education, impressive certifications—all a part of the projection of a perfectly legal, yet often overblown, image of what they can deliver.

Then there is The Bite: a great analytic and service team with true know-how. A system for logically and realistically making steady returns provides Bite.

Pretty boring, huh? Yes, but such a team, like a good old friend, is reliable and trustworthy. Nonetheless, we like to poodle up and go for The Fluff, or feel the strength of a great big German Shepherd's bark. Most of the time, the biggest Bite (the really good advice) comes from the little mutt in the corner who, although often lacking the enchanting exterior, emerges as the one you really trust.

I observe that the illogic comes when we cannot distinguish The Fluff, The Bark & The Bite from each other. We get confused and make wrong moves.

Things are worse in good times when we become less cautious and more prone to believe The Fluffers and The Barkers. Our guard is down. Arguably, we need more protection in good economic times than in bad ones.

If you read my first book, you know I believe we make our own luck when it comes to investing. So, I find it important to focus on the four reasons that you need to put real 'Bite' in your investing in good times as well as bad.

#1. In some ways, things are more uncertain when they are good. Exuberance can bite you in good times.

Today investors are taking more risk in the stock market because of the bullish atmosphere, and the bond market may not be much safer.

A little hike in interest rates could quickly tank a bullish stock market and the bond market even more quickly.

Particularly because so many investors are pre- and post-retirement and are hanging on to their dividend stocks for income instead of going into traditional income vehicles, even a tiny interest rate hike could make them flee to rising yields in bonds or CDs. With so many million investors in that age group, a stampede would kill the indices and the many Exchange Traded Funds (ETFs) which represent them.

The aging of America is an added factor. How will mass retirement affect the market? According to the US General Accenting Office, 700,000 Federal employees alone are eligible to retire by 2016. Many will do so because the bull market helped them recover from 2008 losses. There are 78 million boomers and millions of people over 85. They are not usually heavily in stocks. But, in today's low-interest rate environment, they are stockholders. They can be frightened away from securities by the media, a word from an advisor or a peer.

#2. We also have a unique situation with the valuation of our currency having turned around for the better. We have a strong dollar; and for the first time in a long time, it is a pleasure to take a European vacation. I am not sure how long this will last. With our fiat currency value uncertain, our outlook is uncertain. We are in extraordinary debt. The strength of the dollar is more because of the weakness of other currencies in comparison to our internal economy.

The Euro is no longer supported by the policy of the Swiss Central Banks. We look good by comparison. This may be short-lived.

#3. Then, there is the Foreign Account Tax Compliance Act (FATCA), a law with onerous rules for keeping money offshore. Will that keep money onshore or just make millionaires expatriate?

Good times are not necessarily certain times.

That puts you in a bind. Whom can you trust? Can you really expect a financial advisor to be a historical forecaster as well, understand insurance and manage multi-millions for hundreds of individuals? The short answer is "no," unless they have a stellar team.

We have many high earning executives and entrepreneurial clients whose monetary focus is not always directly connected to their bottom line. They have some additional issues.

Specifically, the high-net-worth individual is preoccupied with taxation, succession planning, leaving a legacy, business development and debt.

I might even say I could write a whole book just on the financial needs of the entrepreneur. But, it is not necessary. A chapter or two will do.

In the end, a good money manager with the right team is needed whether your money was earned from corporate salary, business revenue or inheritance.

The Fluff, The Bark & The Bite

High-net-worth people are bombarded by solicitations to handle their money. The key is to distinguish between The Fluff, The Bark, & The Bite of what is being offered to you. That is why I wrote this update.

Here is the way I see it. What is paramount I call 'The Bite.' The Bite is true knowledge and performance. The kind you can rely on over and over again; the kind that through the years, you learn to trust implicitly. The real deal.

That takes you off of your cycle of illogical decision making based on fear or greed and lets you focus on really good, long-term results. The Bite, as used in this book, also represents proof that an investment strategy is a good one through its actual performance, and the logic of specific proven theories, models and concepts.

'The Bark' is what we all too often experience:

- Media predictions
- Claims about how investments could have performed in the past
- Touts on how great low load funds are simply because they are cheap

Sounds good, but this is not always what makes you money.

Only one thing makes money - buying lower and selling higher.

There is nothing more distracting to an investor than watching a financial channel parading various industry professionals spouting predictions in the most beautiful financial jargon. They speak with such conviction about why a specific investment will or will not pan out. How can you resist taking such sage advice?

Although many of these theories and ideas are interesting and some very legitimate, my bottom line is "Do they have The Bite?" In other words, if I had listened to that pundit's advice time after time for the past five or ten years, what would my return be?

I will take an opinion of a top performing portfolio manager, or an economist associated with a top performing hedge fund, over a beautifully-polished corporate suit with a nice media presence every time.

A well-polished Ivy Leaguer MBA does not impress me as much as a street-smart, hard-working person with a super track record.

And then there is 'The Fluff'. Fluff could be words, actions or a display of marketing materials that get the imaginative part of your brain going. This overshadows what you really need for logical investing, the analytical and logical part of your brain, to digest the information being thrown your way.

Professional speakers are taught that 80% of what an audience remembers is based not on what they say, but how they say it.

How enthusiastic is the presenter? What tone and body language are they using? Sales professionals, too, have spent years refining their sales skills and many do not have The Bite, but they sure sound good.

I cannot tell you how many advisors I have worked with over the past 25 years that drive expensive cars and wear Rolexes in an effort to deliver the "Fluff" or the "Bark." This method of persuasion is not coincidental—the skill has been polished and refined to become irresistible to the client.

You have lost before you ever entered the room. It is like a novice rolling around with a jujitsu black belt. I would be lying to you if I did not tell you that I have been on both sides of that equation, especially in my younger years.

Some of my best friends are in marketing and advertising, and I hope they forgive me, but catchy slogans, a terrific Super Bowl ad, a fancy office and the two-martini lunch might get you some clients, but it won't get you long-lasting ones. Unless they want a celebrity wealth manager for cocktail party talk.

My celebrity bashing and anti-Fluff attitude may seem a bit strange in my case.

My team consists of very high profile people. In fact, I am probably the least known of the folks on my team. And some of my clients are business and sports celebrities, as well.

That really makes my point.

With everyone looking so good, so smart and so accomplished in the world of high net worth wealth management, how do you logically choose an advisor and escape being influenced by The Fluff or The Bark?

In the first *Logical Investing* book, I asked this question, which endures even in these better times:

If you did so well in business or any other moneymaking endeavor, why are you puzzled when it comes to the business of investing?

I know that there are psychological reasons that are likely triggered by the way you were brought up around money, and even cultural reasons that account for your issues around money management. Understanding those reasons might make you feel better, but it will not help you get wealthier or manage your current wealth with ease.

What does help is:

- A great advisor
- A new attitude you can bring to the illogical habits that now surround your investing and wealth management
- A hard shell against The Fluff and The Bark, especially if you are prone to optimism, which so many high achievers are

My clients are very successful by anyone's standards. They are usually business owners or executives of great companies. They have nice families, and they are good providers in the old-fashioned "solid-as-a-rock" meaning of success. Perhaps this describes you as well, or, at least, some aspects of your personal success.

Others of my clients are sportsmen with big incomes and little business experience. Ever since I partnered with football great Wayne Chrebet in 2008, we have become very visible as a high-profile team, written up in *The Wall Street Journal*, *Bloomberg*, *The Daily News* and 26 other well-known media outlets.

THE WALL STREET JOURNAL.

MONDAY, NOVEMBER 29, 2010 © 2010 Dow Jones & Company, Inc. All Rights Reserved.

SPORTS

Chrebet Tackling Life After Football

By SCOTT CACCIOLA

RED BANK, N.J. — For three months during the fall of 2008, Wayne Chrebet co-opted a conference room at the Morgan Stanley building here on Broad Street and studied eight hours a day for his brokerage and securities licenses. He worked from two monstrous books and took practice test after practice test. He had spent 11 seasons sacrificing his body as a wide receiver with the Jets, but this was a challenge of a different sort.

"I'd rather get punched in the face 10 times than study for those tests again," Mr. Chrebet said over lunch this month.

One of the most popular players in Jets history, Mr. Chrebet has reinvented himself as a financial adviser at Morgan Stanley's Red Bank office. At age 37, he has exchanged shoulder pads for finely tailored suits. And he approached those tests — the Series 7, the Series 66 and the Series 31 — the same way he went after the football, fully devoting himself to the task at hand and leaving nothing to chance, even if the process was painful.

He said he enjoys monitoring the market, strategizing with colleagues and "competing" — his word — against advisers at other companies. He still wants to win. And he traveled a long path to reach this phase of his life, finding fulfillment after his football career was preempted by injury.

"The same mental toughness that you saw on the field, he's taken that with him," said Matt Higgins, the Jets' Executive Vice President for business operations.

Mr. Chrebet said he took an interest in managing his own money when Bill Parcells, then the Jets' head coach, pulled him aside early in his career and offered some advice: Save your money because the circus won't be in town forever. His words resonated when Mr. Chrebet signed a seven-year, $17.5-million contract extension before the 2002 season. He became a self-professed CNBC junkie. He also found that many of his teammates were neophytes when it came to financial matters, so he offered guidance here and there. It was more of a hobby, though he could see potential for more.

Jets wide receiver Jerricho Cotchery spent his first two years in the league as Mr. Chrebet's teammate, and he said he was struck by Mr. Chrebet's work ethic and self-discipline. He said he took mental notes on how Mr. Chrebet went about his business.

"His approach to the game, the way he practiced, the way he ran routes — I watched everything about him," Mr. Cotchery said.

It sometimes seemed to Mr. Cotchery that Mr. Chrebet's unheralded background — small guy from a small school — overshadowed the fact that he was excellent at his job. After entering the league as an undrafted free agent out of Hofstra, Mr. Chrebet finished his career with 580 receptions for 7,365 yards and 41 touchdowns. The 1998 season might have been his finest: 75 receptions, 1,083 yards, eight touchdowns.

He also displayed total disregard for his physical health, catch after catch putting him in the path of 225-pound behemoths. In football parlance, he was known for having "guts." He paid a steep price, and he sustained at least six documented concussions. Mr. Chrebet said the damage counting once the total reached double figures. "A lot," he said. "A lot. A lot."

Whatever the number, his last concussion ended his career. On Nov. 6, 2005, Mr. Chrebet went high to grab a pass on third-and-five late in the Jets' 31-26 loss to the San Diego Chargers when free safety Jerry Wilson drove him to the ground, a clean tackle. The back of Mr. Chrebet's helmet slammed against the

(over please)

Former Jet Wayne Chrebet, right, talks with Edward Moldaver at Morgan Stanley's office in Red Bank, N.J.

What I have noticed in the past several years is that these varying backgrounds do not predict who will be accomplished when it comes to managing their own money-- business or sports, heir or stay-at-home Mom--who will be the investment winner?

Page 22

It is not background, but logical thinking that makes the difference. And logical thinking, in the face of so much anxiety, worry, emotion and news panic, is not easy to come by. I have infused this book with better ways to achieve the logical attitude that successful investing demands of anyone, regardless of their training or how they made their money in the first place.

In this book, I take pains to show you exactly how, over the past 25 years, I guided my clients to make their decisions clear and logical.

Most of my clients honor me by giving me authority to trade their portfolio within specific risk constraints. I have the discretion to make decisions for them. So, it is fair to ask why people who are accustomed to being in control would give up control over something as critical as their wealth.

This is why:

Most great business people are simply out of their "turf" when it comes to money management.

Business for them is a separate endeavor from building personal wealth. They put their time into growing the business and channeling their knowledge and industry into business excellence, not into becoming a financial advisor.

Perhaps you remember that even Donald Trump filed for corporate bankruptcy four times, 1991, 1992, 2004, and 2009. All were related to overleveraged casino properties in Atlantic City. However, proper planning and having the proper structures in place allowed Trump to come back to be one of the wealthiest men on the planet. Trump has been a brilliant businessman. Four deals went south; but, hundreds worked out. I'll take those odds anytime.

Donald Trump at Lincoln Day Dinner

Later on, I helped him put a quarter of a billion dollar deal together, which you will read about later in the book.

My business is advising and planning for others. For me, it is no mystery why putting together the right financial plan is a difficult puzzle, even for people who can create the most impressive success in every other way. Yet, we berate ourselves when we cannot be great wealth managers and make the split second financial decisions we need to make, sometimes on a daily basis or many times a day.

Would you be surprised if a financial planning specialist could do surgery or run a chain of dry cleaning stores efficiently? You'd probably say, "You have no business expecting yourself to be able to do that. If you cannot, you are not a failure. It is simply not your field."

Yet, we are expected to know how to make money AND manage it without so much as one course in high school or even college.

It is, therefore, no wonder we buy high and sell low. We are looking for validation before we make decisions.

And there are other reasons that we are puzzled. The markets are simply not moving in the manner that we expect.

Something has changed.

Guaranteed investments pay very little.

Today the interest rates are low, as low as .05% to 2% (if we are lucky). (Ten-year Treasuries are at 2% and short-term rates are close to zero.) So this traditional avenue of conservative investing is tantamount to staying in cash.

Usually, a strategic plan of the Federal Reserve is to adjust interest rates down to 'fix the market' and push stocks up. The technique worked recently as the FED lowered short-term rates and made borrowing to expand a company less costly.

This is related to a term we hear all the time: 'Quantitative Easing.'

What is 'Quantitative Easing?'

Quantitative easing is an unconventional monetary tool used by the Federal Reserve when interest rates are low and there has been a continuous slowdown in the economy. The Federal Reserve lowers rates to stimulate projects and business growth by causing borrowing costs to go down. Hopefully, new initiatives kick-start the sluggish economy. New projects and, therefore, hiring of new employees makes sense when interest rates are low and borrowing is easiest. So quantitative easing is an encouragement by the FED of borrowing to expand growth. A project financed at 7% might not make business sense, but maybe at 5%, 4% or 3% cost of borrowing, it does.

How does the FED do this? The FED buys various longer-term US Treasury bonds depending on the interest rate they want to target. When the FED buys US Treasury securities on the open market, it causes prices of bonds to go up, and yields to go down. Dropping Treasury yields causes a spill over or domino effect on all other rates across the board. Borrowing across the board becomes cheaper, and the economy has a better chance to expand.

As I write this book, there are reports that rates will rise through FED policy in just a few months. If so, there can be lots of losses in the bond market. If rates rise, certain stock prices of highly leveraged companies may also suffer. If a company has a lot of debts, they will eventually have to refinance it at higher rates. Whether short or long term, the debt will cost more diminishing profits and reduce the value of the stock.

More Risk, Less Reward

If you understand 'spreads,' you know that they are very 'compressed' at this time. The spread is the difference between the interest rate of a bond and that which you can get with a US Treasury bond. Blue-chip companies, like Johnson & Johnson, Apple or IBM with the best credit ratings, may currently be issuing bonds at 2 1/2% as compared to 2% on the Treasury. This spread of ½%, for the added risk of lending to a corporation, is very 'thin' or 'compressed.' Now, compare this to BlackBerry or another company with a lower credit rating. It usually would offer a wider spread, but more risk. Today investors are searching for any small increase over US Treasury rates and may be taking on too much risk for too little spread in their reaction to our current low rate environment. Said another way, spreads are compressed.

What it means to you is that the Barkers and Fluffers are out in force offering high-risk panaceas of which you must be wary.

Bond Math

Here is an actual email I sent my clients concerned with bond interest.

Before you read it, look at the below chart which shows 10 and 30 year Treasury yields over the past ten years. Fixed rate bond prices have an inverse relationship to rising and falling rates.

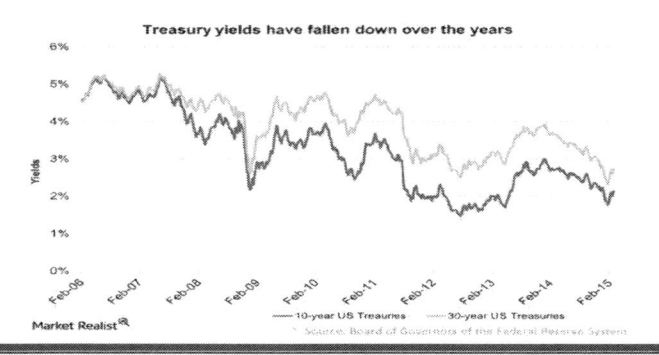

-----Original Message-----
From: Moldaver, Ed: WIM
Sent: Monday, May 18, 2015 9:44 AM
Subject: FW: Bond Math

Dear Clients,

My team and I have been advising all of you to reduce exposure to longer-term fixed-income bonds. In fact, I dedicated a Chapter in my book.

The risk reward was and still is not there. Instead as you know, we have been accumulating variable or floating rate securities and certain fixed to float securities. These securities are either currently floating or will float at some time in the future at a spread above LIBOR. In other words if the LIBOR is .25% and your bond is LIBOR + a spread of 300 bp (basis points), you will get 3.25%. If LIBOR rises to 2, you will get 2%+ 3%=5%. Rising rates damage fixed-income bond prices, not so for variable and floating rate bonds.

Obviously the markets discount the news ahead of time and these bonds start going up way before the LIBOR starts to move. We have been accumulating these investments for over a year and a half now and are sitting with nice profits. For example; JP Morgan 7.9% fixed until 4-30-2018 and then floats to LIBOR +347 bp, we were buying between 100 and 105. It currently is at 112 and traded as high as 117. We received the 7.9% coupon and the appreciation of 7-12%. (see graph)

Conversely a 10 year Treasury that was yielding 1.7%, since May 1st now yields 2.4%. That bond has a duration of 9. That means for every 1% move in yield, the bond moves 9% in the opposite direction. The 10 year Treasury lost 5.7% in principle since May 1st. (see graph 2). A 10 year corporate fixed rate bond acts in a very similar fashion.

Within our Strategic Income and Dividend model we had similar structures, but rather than buying individual securities, we were buying Closed End Funds such as "ARK" Blackrock. It invests in Senior Floating Rate bank notes. We started buying this position in 2011, when it was out of favor and trading at 7-10% discount to its Net Asset Value (see graph 3). In other words we were paying $90-93 for $100 of securities. We sold the entire position in March. We received a total return of 23%, annualizing 13% inclusive of interest and dividends from the fund.

The bottom line: We will be sticking with low duration & variable rate bonds. As and if rates continue to move up, we will be entertaining the idea of longer duration and higher coupon securities. We will also be looking to initiate these positions, many of which are starting to trade at deep discounts to their Net Asset Values, within the Closed End Fund universe through my Strategic Income and Dividend Model.

I hope this helps explain the recent turmoil taking place in our bond market. Please feel free to give me a call with any questions or concerns that you may have.

Ed Moldaver

Are you a target for Fluffers and Barkers?

When the investment environment is tough, is just when The Fluffers and The Barkers come out of the woodwork. They have high claim, innovative ideas that sound like panaceas. But, is there any Bite behind their suggestions?

You are if:

- You do not trust yourself because you have made bad decisions in the past.
- You do not trust the financial planning industry because it has made bad decisions.

- You are averse to current income vehicles because they pay next to nothing, and you are susceptible to taking credit risks in exchange for high interest.

- You have lost faith in the US dollar, maybe even the US position as a world power, and are susceptible to offshore schemes (very different from offshore strategies which often have great Bite).

Sometimes we create our own Bark, because we believe a bit too much in our own investment acumen.

What do most people do when their more conservative stocks take a beating and bonds pay next to nothing? They flee to LESS conservative, riskier investments.

Investors run to bonds with greater credit risk and higher returns, or they run to longer maturities that pay more but have much greater interest rate risk. A 20-year, zero-coupon bond will move 20% in value for every 1% move in interest rates. A 10 year Treasury with a 2% yield will move 9% in the opposite direction if there is a 1% interest rate change. A 30 year Treasury with a 2.5% yield will move 21% in the opposite direction if there is a 1% interest rate change.

This is not disastrous if you have the know-how to analyze the bonds and protect yourself. This is a new piece of the puzzle that no layman investor can easily figure out.

Is asset allocation Bark or Bite?

Most models for wealth management and investment planning are based on investing in a set allocation of asset classes, so that when one investment zigs, the other zags, and the whole portfolio comes into balance eventually. If not, you rebalance it.

In fact, most financial advisors, our Group included, study how assets interact with each other and rely on those past market behaviors to make the zigzag allocation.

Historically, major asset classes, like stocks vs. bonds, could be counted upon to balance each other. When one went up, the other went down.

Currently, major asset classes still balance each other, but they go up and down together at different paces, making the art of asset allocation more complex.

For example, as I mentioned before, if the US economy is struggling and stock prices go down, the FED lowers rates, bond yields tumble and prices of bonds go up. In short, low rates stimulate the economy. Our companies make more profits as money is put into company growth, and prices of stocks rise on increased demand. The FED then raises rates, and the cycle repeats again over and over. So, it is logical to own both stocks and bonds to stabilize your portfolio.

But, different asset classes are not correlating quite so perfectly these days.

When the Dow (the 30 stocks in the Dow Jones Industrial Average that are the bell-weathers of the market as a whole) went from 13,000 to 7,000 in 2009, investors were shocked. The Dow was at 14,000 in 2007. At the time of this writing, we are at 18,000. But, unlike 2009, 2007, or most any other time, we are at virtually 0% short-term interest rates.

At this writing, 10 year Treasuries are at 2%. Shall it go down to .5%?

When lowered stock markets cannot be bolstered by lowering interest rates, we lose a curative tool that allowed us to rely on a simple two-asset class asset allocation for balance. Just owning stocks and bonds no longer gives the balance we want to achieve.

Sometimes the true nature of an investment is obscured by its complexity. I call a complex investment design that looks great but hides inherent flaws a Barker.

Here is an example of an investment we like but that can be complex. That investment is the commodity ETF, Exchange Traded Funds.

Let us look at natural gas, as an example, because it is often in the news these days. Say you think that natural gas will go up in value and want to invest there. You buy an ETF that invests in natural gas stocks, or so you think. You choose to invest through an ETF because it has the benefit of being traded at the value of the investments it holds at any given time, as it is constantly re-evaluated.

Mutual funds in natural gas, by contrast, are evaluated only once a day around 4 p.m., so you might have lost the value of the high for that day, if you want to sell or the low if you want to buy. But, with an ETF, you can make a transaction at any given time and get the real-time valuation.

So far, so good.

Now, let us posit that natural gas goes up just as you thought it would. But, whoa, your natural gas ETF went down! How did that happen? You understand too late that the ETF did not own natural gas company stock but instead futures on natural gas. The prices of those commodity contracts roll and are traded in a different market from the stock of natural gas companies. They are part of the more volatile futures market. You bought something more volatile and complex than you anticipated.

The number 1 rule of Bite - If you do not understand an investment, find someone who does and can analyze it for you. Someone who is not compensated by commission, but is a true wealth manager, compensated by making your portfolio grow.

Here is how looking only at Bite and forgetting Fluff and Bark could save your financial future.

At the time of the 2008 collapse of companies too big to fail, there were numerous high interest rate notes, bonds and more complex income vehicles being sold. The fate of those securities and the investors that bought them were not all the same.

For example, Lehman notes ended up at zero, Bear Stearn's notes temporarily traded at 20 cents on the dollar, until JP Morgan bought them out, and the notes and bonds traded back to $100.

Here is one piece of advice I can give you, if you want to figure out the puzzle.

Every stock and every corporate bond is really an investment in the company. Look at and evaluate the company first and the market second.

Even Federal government securities are an investment in a government. Evaluate the stability and economics of the government first, before you invest in it, even when that government is the United States of America.

Such analysis has Bite.

Is Portfolio Risk Analysis Fluff, Bark or Bite? You may be surprised by the answer.

I trust what I can quantify. What will an act of terrorism do to your portfolio? What will every 1% change in a bond yield mean to your bottom line?

With the perfecting of computer programs in the financial industry, everyone is offering a portfolio analysis that shows you what elements in the markets and the world would impact your portfolio.

This may sound like Fluff - a way to get you in the door to open an investment relations conversation. That may be so in many cases; but motive aside, these stress test analytics have Bite.

With non-market factors like politics, foreign central bank policy and more affecting global stocks and domestic bonds as never before, you do need to stress test your portfolio. We devoted an entire chapter to this in *Logical Investing*, much of which you will find updated in Chapter 14 of this book.

For now, see how bond interest rates can stress your portfolio:

Often the duration of the bonds you hold will dictate the risk you take when yields rise and fall. Let us look at the impact of interest rate change on two portfolios with similar quality bonds but different duration factors:

To analyze a portfolio logically, we use Portfolio Risk Analysis. We quantify, quantify, quantify. You may be able to withstand more risk than you think, and make more interest than you think. But, risk will panic you if you act only on emotions without logic.

I like to use the analogy of a homeowner living on the oceanfront overlooking a beautiful beach. But, tides and weather may flood the house once every 25 years. Sure, that is a disaster; but if you have flood insurance and you are aware of the possibilities, you get decades of good living. If you bail out at the first raindrop, you can never take advantage of the benefits of beach and ocean view living. It makes as little sense to "dump" your home right after a flood as it does to sell a good business in bad times.

If you can wait out a market and have good security backing an investment, do not sell. Corporate bond ownership is just lending to a business; do not bail out when the business is good and the market is bad.

Chapter 2

The Bark and The Bite of Financial History

I enjoy reading what investment pundits of the past had to say and comparing their times with ours. I found a gem of a book on EBay. Here's a quote I live by:

"Almost every general idea of speculation is the exact reverse of the truth. Sometimes this is caused by false reasoning but, most frequently, by the innate false appearances of the market quotations. For example, greatest activity and interest in a market occur around top prices, while dullness and stagnation are invariable when properties are unreasonably low in price." The Pitfalls of Speculation, by Thomas Gibson, The Moody Corporation, 1906

A lot has happened historically to the markets since my first book, *Logical Investing,* was published. Here is the way I see some important market stressors of recent history:

1. The enactment of Dodd-Frank to restrict banking transactions and sharpen reporting, in light of the over-enthusiastic credit offerings to unqualified borrowers that nearly tanked the real estate and mortgage market.

2. Currently, there is low liquidity in the bond market. Banks and brokerage firms have 1/10th the inventory on hand compared to 2007. This is related to Dodd-Frank; as under the legislation, banks are discouraged to take risks.

3. Quantitative easing - lowering interest rates to stimulate the economy and raise stock prices.

4. The use of quantitative easing in Europe to bolster the economy.

5. The addition of the Yuan as a world reserve currency that may weaken the dollar.

6. The Swiss refusal to support the Euro despite its promise to do so.

7. FATCA, requiring more onerous reporting of overseas accounts.

8. The recession of 2008-2009 and the fortunate bull market which followed.

Despite the commotion of history, nothing much has changed in human behavior and reaction. Check out this excerpt from the first *Logical Investing*. It requires repeating and taking to heart. You will see just how much Bark affects us in our decision making.

When the Dow Jones Industrial Average moves 100 to 150 points, I have a habit of sending e-mails to my clients giving a macro view of the markets. It can be these macro events that cause you to act illogically. Look at the history of 74 reasons people failed to invest over the past 70 years.

Today we can add several other events, such as the bailouts, the Gulf War, 9/11 and various elections. You will see that $10,000 invested in the stock market (Standard & Poor's 500 Index) in January 1934, with no further buying or selling, would have been worth more than $21 million before fees at the end of 2007. What a legacy! We can slice and dice the market over any 20-year period and get good results. So, it is not only past market performance but, also, current scary circumstances that create illogical thought.

74 Reasons Why People did not Invest in the Stock Market

1934 — Depression

1935— Spanish Civil War

1936— Economy Still Struggling

1937— Recession

1938— War Cloud Gathers

1939— War in Europe

1940 —France Falls

1941—Pearl Harbor

1942 —Wartime Price Controls

1943 —Industry Mobilizes

1944 —Consumer Goods Shortage

1945 —Post-War Recession Predicted

1946 —Dow Tops 200 - Market Too High

1947 —Cold War Begins

1948 —Berlin Blockade

1949 —Russia Explodes A-Bomb

1950 —Korean War

1951 —Excess Profits Tax

1952 —US Seizes Steel Mills

1953 —Russia Explodes A-Bomb

1954 —Dow Tops 300—Market Too High

1955 —Eisenhower Illness

1956 —Suez Crisis

1957 —Russia Launches Sputnik

1958 —Recession

1959 —Castro Seizes Power in Cuba

1960 —Russia Downs U-2 Plane

1961 —Berlin Wall Erected

1962 —Cuban Missile Crisis

1963 —Kennedy Assassinated

1964 —Gulf of Tonkin

1965 —Civil Rights Marches

1966 —Vietnam War Escalates

1967 —Newark Race Riots

1968 —USS Pueblo Seized

1969 —Money Tightens - Markets Fall

1970 —Cambodia Invaded - Vietnam War Spreads

1971 —Wage Price Freeze

1972 —Largest US Trade Deficit Ever

1973 —Energy Crisis

1974 —Steepest Market Drop in Four Decades

1975 —Clouded Economic Prospects

1976 —Economy Recovers Slowly

1977 —Market Slumps

1978 — Interest Rates Rise

1979 — Oil Prices Skyrocket

1980 — Interest Rates at All-Time High

1981—Steep Recession Begins

1982—Worst Recession in 40 Years

1983—Market Hits New High

1984—Record Federal Deficits

1985—Economic Growth Slows

1986—Dow Nears 2,000

1987—Record-Setting Market Decline

1988—Election Year

1989—October "Mini Crisis"

1990—Persian Gulf Crisis

1991—Communism Tumbles with the Berlin Wall

1992—Global Recession

1993—Health Care Reform

1994—FED Raises Interest Rates Six Times

1995—Dow Tops 5,000

1996—Dow Tops 6,400

1997—Hong Kong Reverts to China

1998—Asian Flu

1999 —Y2K Scare

2000 —Tech Bubble Burst

2001 —9/11 Terrorist Attacks

2002 —Recession

2003 —War in Iraq

2004 —Rising Interest Rates

2005 —Hurricane Katrina

2006 —Real Estate Peaks

2007 —Liquidity Crisis & Subprime Lending

Source: Atalanta Sosnoff; ASC Company Research

*Dow Jones Industrial Average: The most widely used indicator of the overall condition of the stock market, a price-weighted average of 30 actively traded blue-chip stocks, primarily

industrials. The 30 stocks are chosen by the editors of the Wall Street Journal *(which is published by Dow Jones & Company), a practice that dates back to the beginning of the century. The Dow was officially started by Charles Dow in 1896, at which time it consisted of only 11 stocks. The Dow is computed using a price-weighted indexing system, rather than the more common market cap-weighted indexing system. Simply put, the editors at WSJ add up the prices of all the stocks and then divide by the number of stocks in the index. (In actuality, the divisor is much higher today in order to account for stock splits that have occurred in the past.)*

*S&P 500: Widely regarded as the best single gauge of the US equities market, this world-renowned index includes a representative sample of 500 leading companies in leading industries of the US economy. Although the S&P 500 focuses on the large-cap segment of the market, with over 80% coverage of US equities, it is also an ideal proxy for the total market.

Performance Results are derived from the return of the S&P 500 Index including the reinvestment of dividends and interest and does not include a reduction of fees.

© 2009 Morgan Stanley Smith Barney LLC. Member SIPC. Consulting Group and Investment Advisory Services are businesses of Morgan Stanley Smith Barney LLC.

History Can Be Very Dangerous Fluff

Here are three graphs which show the performance of the S&P 500 from March 1975-1985 with an annual return of 12.8%; March 1995-2005 with an annual return of 10.76%; and March 2005-2015 with an annual return of 7.9995%. Even if we calculated since the 1930's depression we would have an annualized Rate of Return of 8%.

Think of all the historical events that frightened or otherwise motivated investors during these time periods. Think of how many transactions were erroneously based on these events, instead of the value of the underlying investments.

The key point is that despite all of the external happenings and historic change the S&P earned 8%-9% annually if you had the stomach to stay in the game over a long period of time. Today, those who wish to balance their portfolio should remain 65% in stocks. (If you are very pessimistic, 35%.)

Dollar cost averaging into an index works. We do that on a more sophisticated level with individual stocks, funds and hedge funds. Right now we're doing a little more of that with energy stocks because they took a recent hit. Money markets are too low yielding for our taste.

When it comes to equities our game is clear. We get the best of the best and add to them. For clients who have a 20-year plan, look the other way during your correction, as we will most likely be buying low for you. We see this as an opportunity while others see it as a crisis.

Our strategy makes you part owner of the best companies in the world. The best part of that is someone else is running your business!

Of course, as you near retirement, you'll want less and less volatility; and you strive for a more income-generating portfolio with greater balance.

We don't overlook annuities. The concept can be good. Stay in the market with downside guarantees. People understand the concept; but, they rarely understand the investment itself. It is not unlike buying a basket of mutual funds that have special features and guarantees. You pay for the guarantees that secure against market loss; but, that may be worth it to you as you near retirement.

In the long run, my message is simple. Stocks make money over time, one way or another. Let us watch them for you and make sure that your fears don't tank your long-term profits.

Although, over all, this time the market returned 8-12% consistently; you cannot time a market unless you have the stomach to act on bad news. Even then you must act when the news is very bad and sell when the news is very good. Few people can do this year after year.

Tinker with a stock portfolio just because you are uncomfortable with volatility, and you are likely to be a loser. But, many of us have a temperament that sends us into cash just to reduce vulnerability.

That is why we structure a portfolio according to personality and yet make our selections logical, so every investor is comfortable enough to understand their long-term plan and not react unduly to short-term moves.

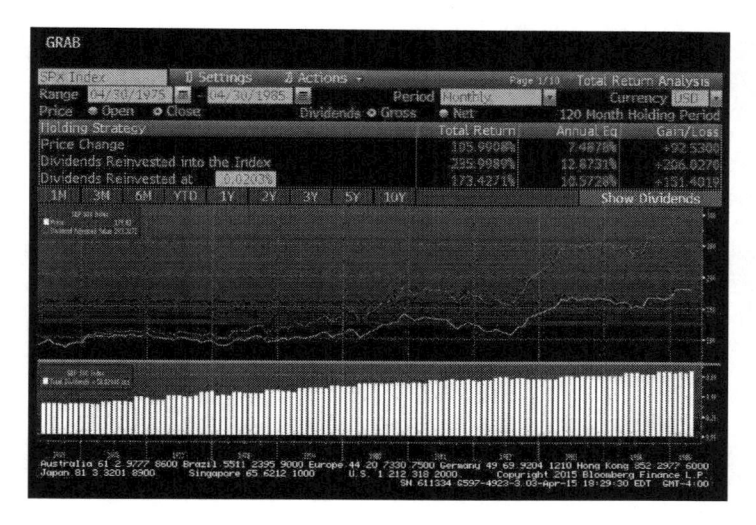

10 Year Annualized Market Gain
1975-1985--12.8%

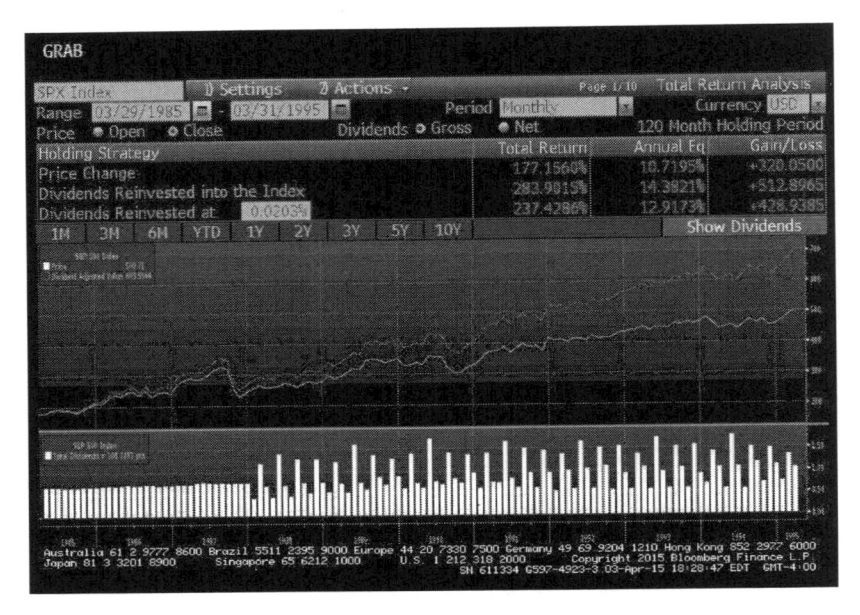

**10 Year Annualized Market Gain
1985-1995--14.3%**

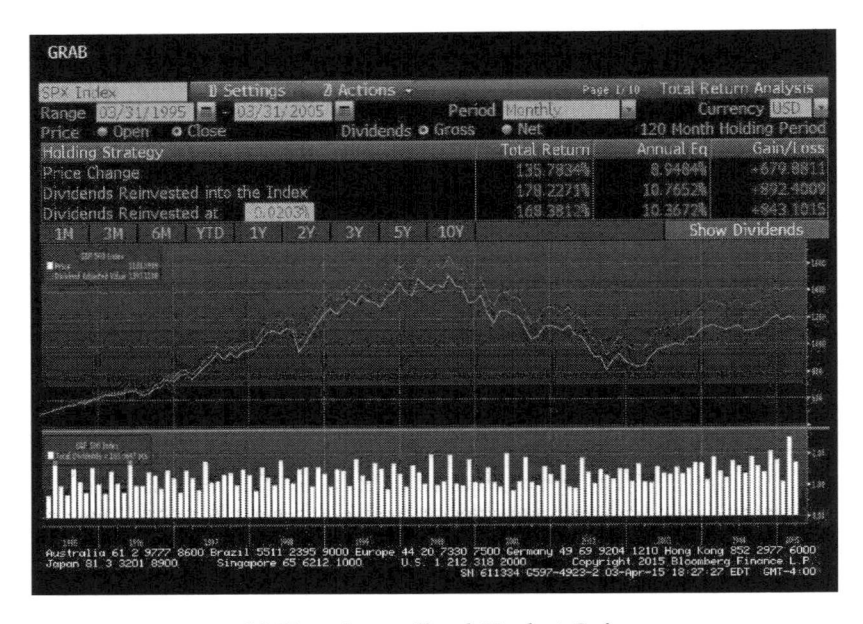

**10 Year Annualized Market Gain
1995-2005--10.26%**

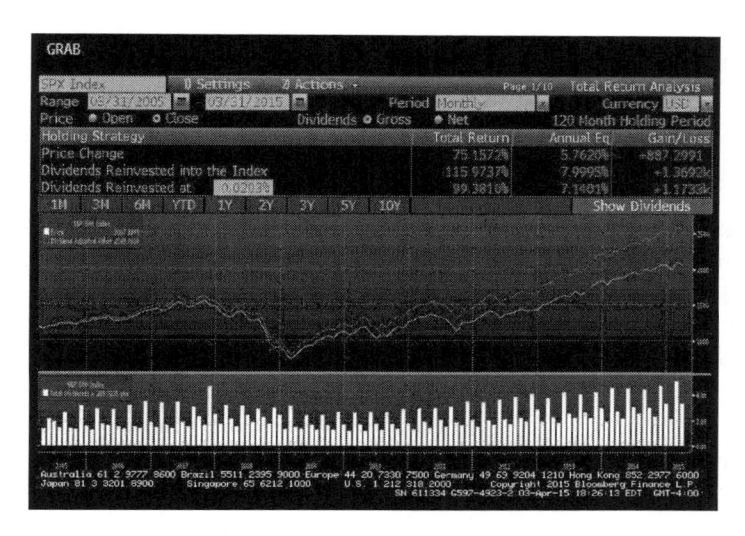

**10 Year Annualized Market Gain
2005-2015--7.9%**

Big Bark! Or, Death to Market Timing!

So, should your grandmother or great-grandfather have invested in the market in 1954, or even 1934, if they had had money to do so? With hindsight, of course, the answer is yes. But what were their circumstances then? What are yours now?

It matters whether you are 10 to 20 years before or right at retirement as to what your best move is during the economic shifts that affect us all. That is why I do not subscribe to one-size-fits-all theories of market timing or even one asset allocation mix.

In general, I believe in the efficiency of the markets in the long term. In the short term, it's a different story.

But, I do not necessarily subscribe to any type of market timing strategies, such as, "Stochastics" (a method of trying to predict stock price trends by finding past bottoms and top prices of a stock and comparing them to current prices), or

"50 day moving averages" (a method of analyzing stock price trends to predict future results by tracking the average price of a stock over the prior 50-day period, readjusting each day to predict the price trend).

These types of individual stock trading formulas or theories or strategies, whatever you want to call them, are done with no regard as to who you are or to the fundamentals of the company whose stock they track. That is not good enough for me.

It may be quantifiable, but it is not logical. If it worked, all you would have to do is write a program to let a computer track trades and make a trillion dollars. So far, no one has achieved that in any meaningful way.

In Chapters 8 and 17 and in other parts of the book, I will clue you in on some techniques for buying and selling that rely on market analysis. But, I cannot entirely rely on them. Why? Because they require an efficient market to be 100% predictive; and sometimes the markets are not efficient.

In March of 2009, we made 44% on safe municipal bonds because of the inefficiency of the market. How? We researched municipal bond Closed End Funds for our clients and identified that while their value went down, the value of the underlying bonds in the portfolio did not change as much. If you looked for it, you could buy a share in a bond fund at 44% less than the Net Asset Value of the bonds it held. If you were using an automatic strategy, you would miss this opportunity.

Here Is The Bite in a Nutshell:

When you buy a stock, you own part of the company. When you buy a bond, you lend to a company. The fundamentals of the company are most important. For each company in which you want to invest or to lend, ask:

- What are their assets?

- What is their management team like?

- What is their research and development like?

- Perhaps you are thinking that I am a value investor; that is pretty close to how I see things, and it is logical.

Take a look back at the 74 historical reasons why people did not buy in bad times or crisis times. Most people avoided the markets out of fear, which Barks at you almost every time there is trouble.

Most were opportunities, if you had the nerve. I have one overall philosophic view. If you live in a country that has a 100% track record of recovering from bad times, as we have, start to look at each macro crisis as a possible opportunity to invest.

The Barkiest Barkers of All: The Media

Before we leave the issue of macro events, let us look at events that really do not take place—the non-events that make us illogical about investing.

Look, I forgive the press. They need news, and once in a while, they make it up or, at least, report it in a way that makes for a great news cycle but lousy investing.

Perhaps it is best to take your financial advice from people who make investment decisions for a living, not from people who report news for a living. Sometimes it is just better not to react to news at all and wait things out, rather than to be

Conversation with Steve Forbes and Jimmy Lee

Page 45

proactive every time a news story hits.

I recently had the pleasure of meeting Steve Forbes of *Forbes Magazine*. He joked that when people asked his Dad to suggest an investment tip, Malcolm Forbes would reply, "It is a lot more profitable to give investment advice than to take it."

> *"Too great facilities for obtaining information and executing orders, is, to the ordinary trader, of no advantage, as frequently a source of loss. (The accounts mentioned above show the most intelligent trading to have been done by traders who were without facilities to interfere with their own original plans through fright or confusion.)"*
>
> **The Pitfalls of Speculation, by Thomas Gibson**
> **The Moody Corporation, 1906**

Buyer's remorse is inflamed when the media floods you with information - you get off track if you react to every press release or commentary. Most people begin to pay attention to the money media after they have made a decision not before.

It is only human nature to look back and find reasons to regret and question. If you made a smart decision based on your values, your needs, your net worth and your personality, no news is good news if it is going to throw you off track.

Words of wisdom from Wharton, again: "Encourage the client to ignore the media (or view it simply as entertainment) and to focus instead on making wise financial decisions and sticking with the long – term plan for achieving all that is important to him or her."

Investment gains do not go in a straight line, they are **"Uneven by Nature."** It is very important to look at progress over time in personal investing; news reports look at minute-to-minute results. Today, we not only have 24-hour reporting, we have 24-hour markets. That is why, for example, the US market can be momentarily impacted by what is going on in Asia and five minutes later, everything has turned around, because the impact is already old news.

That does not mean that we should never act on catastrophic events that we feel are real. But, with the logical response structure we have set up for our clients, they are fully prepared.

For example, let us say a news report comes in that stock prices are down 20% and bond prices are worse—down 40%.

Do you act or stay put? And, if you do act, how?

That is a trick question because the right answer needs to include what alternative is available to you.

In a real-life example, we had a General Electric bond available that was 40% off its par price; in a few years, it would be called at par. The client also had a stock with a 20% loss if she sold. We did take the loss, but we bought the bond at 40% off par price and made over 67% overall when it was called at par. After we owned the replacement bonds for a while, the price went back up from 60 to 100, so we could have sold even before the call.

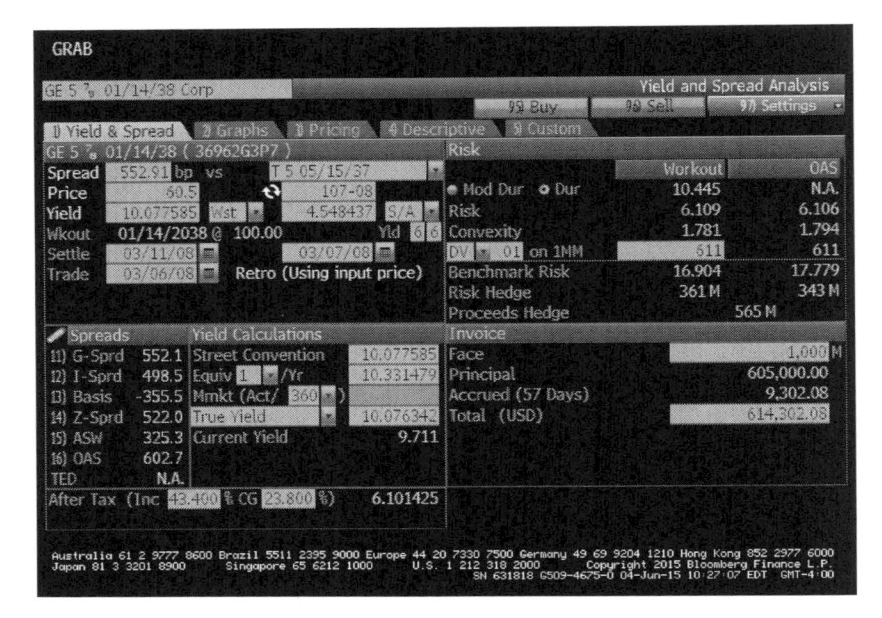

General Electric

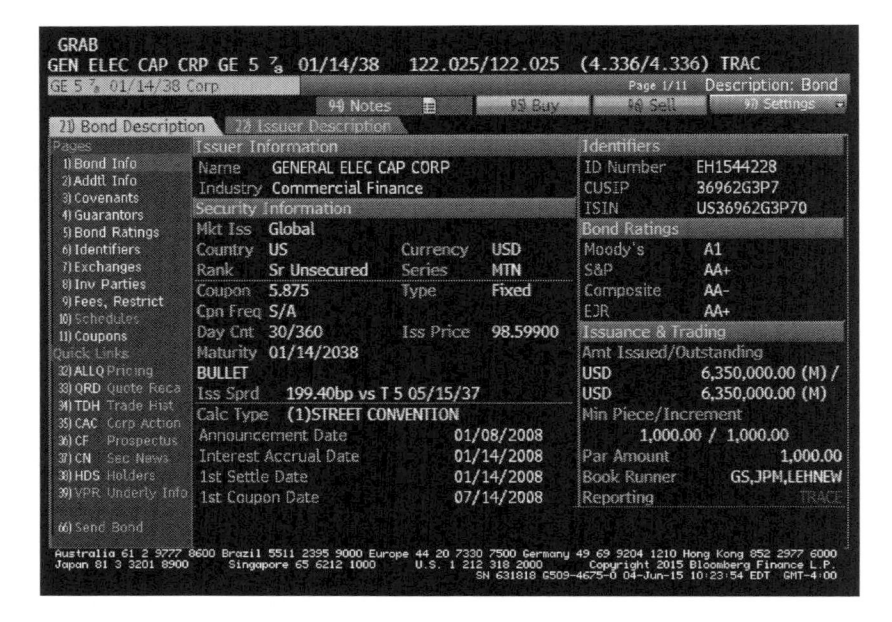

General Electric

General Electric

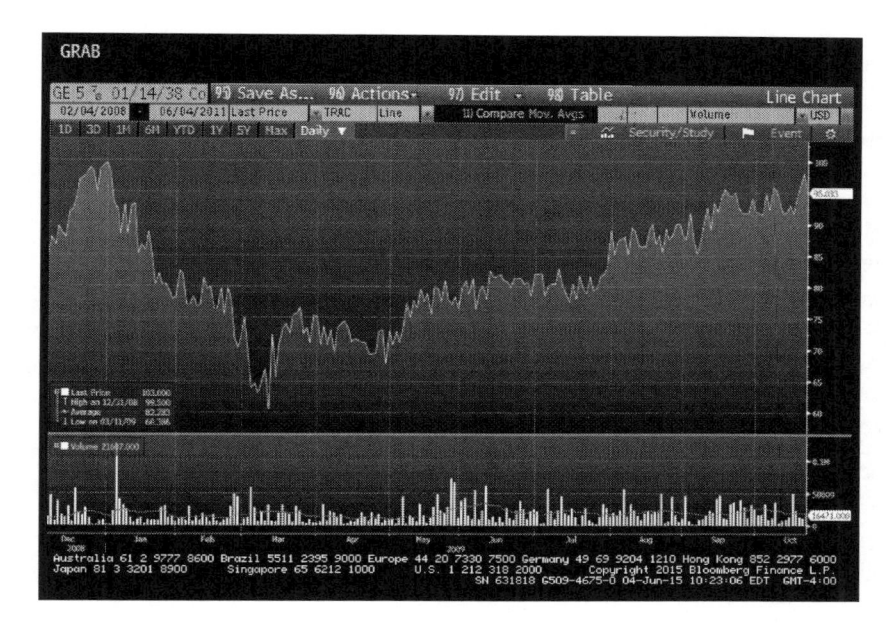

Be cognizant of the logic of the 'Pecking Order of Safety,' which can dictate what you want to own when protection from corporate bankruptcy is a factor:

When there is trouble with a company that portends its bankruptcy, you may actually be able to do well. The 'Pecking Order' of safety, who gets paid in bankruptcy, goes this way:

- Secured loans
- General obligation bonds
- Junior or subordinate bonds
- Preferred stocks
- Common stocks

The further down the pecking order you go, the higher the risk and the greater the reward should be. If you believe that a company in trouble will recover, consider a secured bond rather than a riskier stock. Such companies usually are not credit worthy through the usual channels and will pay bond buyers high rates to get the cash they need to stay afloat.

Sounds logical? It was for one of our clients who did not need immediate liquidity. Of course, we might have done something different if we had known that she needed liquidity and might have to cash in before the maturity date.

Before we leave the issue of responding to a macro event, I want to look at a feature of decision making that is often overlooked and how understanding it changed the way I do business big time.

During our regular progress meetings with clients, we ask about their personal news. It is important that your family news, like the birth of a child or grandchild, the receipt of an inheritance, or the failing health of your parents be "broadcasted" to us. Your news is what is important for logical decision making about your investments.

Sometimes non-financial news is more important than financial news.

If you are on the board of a charity and that charity has problems, you may have liability. If you have investments offshore, and there is a weakness in a country in which you have a position, we need to act. Your mind map review will alert us to the issues that go beyond your investing.

Many of our clients have more than one home, and many of them are in areas like Florida or Maine that are seriously affected by the weather. It seems strange to say, but news about the weather may have a more direct impact on your wealth than the Monday night news or the financial gurus' and pundits' minute-to-minute market analysis.

Reaction Time

Let us look at the aspect of how fast you can make an investment decision, or REACTION TIME. How quickly you can react to a crisis or an opportunity very well may dictate your ultimate results. That brings up the issue of how quickly your broker can act, as well. With a non-discretionary account, he or she needs to consult with you before making a trade. With a discretionary account, he or she can act without that consultation.

When you open an account with anyone, consider the limitations on him or her and on yourself to act quickly.

Here is the way it used to go with our office in the 1990's, and still does for most advisors. When an economic event moved us so much that we knew an overall change in our clients' portfolios was necessary, our window of opportunity was time-limited if we wanted to make trades at optimal prices. But, most of our clients had opened non-discretionary accounts. In other words, we needed their permission to buy, sell or otherwise trade in any way.

We had no trading authority. If an advisor has 100 non-discretionary accounts, he or she must call 100 people to get trading permission. If you decide on the non-discretionary account where you must be consulted, ask, "Who gets the first call?" How would you like to be number 100 on the call list?

Heaven forbid you are on vacation. What happens to the last client to be called? He or she might sell at a lower price as the value tumbles down. And if the client is unavailable—forget it.

In 2008, I fixed the problem. I made my own logical decision to take on mostly accounts where my clients sign a trading discretion document under which I act as a Registered Investment Advisor on their behalf. I call whenever there is time. And I trade only within the parameters that we set up at the beginning of our relationship. I continue to monitor adherence to our parameters during review sessions.

Some of my usual parameters are:

- No more than 5% exposure to any one company
- No industry representing more than 20% of the portfolio
- At least seven industries in a portfolio

In that way, my clients and I never lose control of the portfolio and keep it balanced and moving. We can take profits in a split second, and we do not wait out a loss to the bitter end. We can act together, or I can act for them. But, neither of us is at the mercy of the clock.

Chapter 3

How The Fluff and The Bark Affects Your Psyche

With your permission, I would like to tell you a few personal things about myself, in order to make you more comfortable thinking about the personal life experiences that cause you to react less than logically when it comes to making investment and other financial decisions.

Cognitive tests prove that when people need to make decisions on incomplete information, which happens all the time with investing since we cannot predict the future, we fill in the blanks from our own background.

In fact, in our office, we have a Longevity Group; and we know that our older clients have a very different decision-making process from our younger ones. They have a longer life background from which to draw. Cognitive scientists say that as we age, we may lose some fluid intelligence (we think slower) but we gain crystallized intelligence (we are wiser).

Who you are, from your age to your education, to the triumphs and losses of your past, impacts whether or not you apply logic to investing.

Now a bit about me:

I have completed several executive-level programs and gained certifications. One is The Wharton School Certified Investment Management Program. I also received my Certified Portfolio Manager (CPM) designation from the Academy of Certified Portfolio Managers taught by the faculty of Columbia University. I am currently on the Board of Trustees of the Academy of Certified Portfolio Managers.

But, please do not get the wrong idea. I am still the kid that emigrated from Kiev in the Ukraine, near the Dnieper River, and started my life in the United States in 1978, when I was 12 years old.

I began my career in finance as a runner in the commodities pits at the World Trade Center while attending college. Since then, I have spent close to 25 years managing wealth for affluent families, corporations, and institutions. I guess I cared about money so much because I never had any.

I managed wealth for clients at Barclays, Morgan Stanley Smith Barney and at Bear Stearns' exclusive Private Client Services Group. While at Bear Sterns, I became one of the firm's youngest to earn the title of Senior Managing Director.

Regardless of where my office is associated, I bring my team and client base with me.

Over the past 15 years, my clients and firms paid me over $100 million to represent them in the markets and oversee their family's wealth.

I became a member of the Morgan Stanley Smith Barney Business Owner Executive Council, an invitation-only program reserved for the top 2% of financial advisors who focus their practice on helping small- and middle-market business owners. In addition, I have been instrumental in introducing and coordinating investment banking and real estate deals for my clients.

In an article titled "America's Best," *Barron's* named me the #1 financial advisor in New Jersey in their annual list of America's Top 1000 Advisors: 2012 State-by-State.

I have consistently ranked in the top ten on that list in prior years. In 2009, I was named as one of the Top 100 Financial Advisors in America as published in *Registered Rep.* In 2012, *Barron's* ranked me in the top 100 in the USA as well.

I know that many advisors wonder what special 'magic' I have. No magic, I just started my career making 300 cold calls a day. Now, that I have one of the nation's largest established practices, I do not work one minute fewer than I did in my hungry days. I just work on the clients' business with my terrific team.

Of course, I work in an industry subject to mergers and acquisitions. Many times I need to make stressful decisions to move on so that I can 'cocoon' myself in an environment which offers my team the expertise I insist on for my clients. Wherever I take my practice, I always maintain the same level of excellence.

How else could I assist Donald Trump in building the Trump Ocean Club in Panama City? With the blessing of Ace Greenberg, I facilitated Trump's needed quarter of a billion bond deal.

The Ocean Club in Panama

It was the #1 *Barron's* ranking that compelled me to write this book. Although, I frequently contribute articles to *The Wall Street Journal, Barron's,* and *Registered Rep,* and I appear on radio and in numerous local media outlets, this book is my chance to let you in on how we get results with no space or editorial constraints. Thanks for reading!

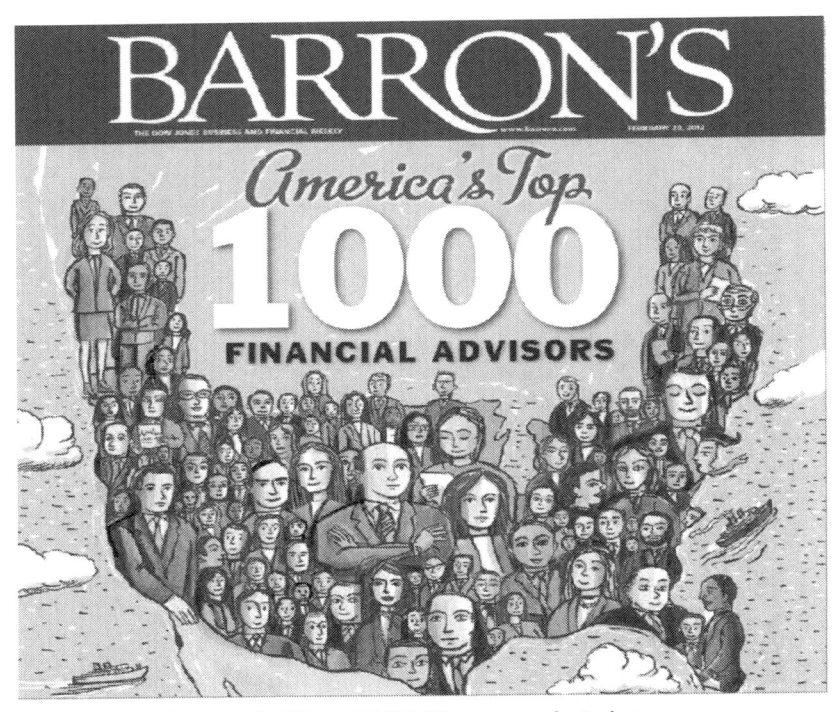

The 2012 *Barron's* Top 1000 Financial Advisors

Rankings based on assets under management, revenue generated for advisors' firms, quality of practices and other factors.
N=New.

NEW JERSEY—RANKED #1

1. 5. Ed Moldaver   Morgan Stanley Smith Barney   Red Bank   •   •   •   1,350   4   10

Source: Barron's "Top 1,000 Advisors," February 20, 2012, as identified by Barron's magazine, using quantitative and qualitative criteria and selected from a pool of over 4,000 nominations. Advisors in the Top 1,000 Financial Advisors have a minimum of seven years of financial services experience. Qualitative factors include, but are not limited to, compliance record, interviews with senior management, and philanthropic work. Investment performance is not a criterion. The rating may not be representative of any one client's experience and is not indicative of the financial advisor's future performance. Barron's is a registered trademark of Dow Jones & Company, L.P. All rights reserved. Neither Morgan Stanley Smith Barney LLC nor its Financial Advisors pay a fee to Barron's in exchange for the rating.

Source: Barron's "Top 100 Financial Advisors," April 16, 2012. Barron's is a registered trademark of Dow Jones & Company, L.P. All rights reserved. Barron's "Top 100 Financial Advisors" bases its ratings on qualitative criteria: professionals with a minimum of 7 years financial services experience, acceptable compliance records, client retention reports, customer satisfaction, and more.

Page 56

Know the Barron's rating system: Financial Advisors are quantitatively rated based on varying types of revenues and assets advised by the financial professional, with weightings associated for each. Because individual client portfolio performance varies and is typically unaudited, this rating focuses on customer satisfaction and quality of advice. For more information on rating methodology, go to http://online.barrons.com/report/top financial advisors or contact Barron's Associate Editor, Matt Barthel, at matthew.barthel@barrons.com. The rating may not be representative of any one client's experience because it reflects a sample of all of the experiences of the Financial Advisor's clients.

America's Best

By Steve Garmhausen

The following has been excerpted

[Excerpted article text about top financial advisors, including profile of Ed Moldaver, New Jersey—Ranked #1, former Bear Stearns advisor now with Morgan Stanley. Typical profile table shows Total Assets $1.4 bil, Typical Account $4 mil, Typical Net Worth $10 mil.]

Source: Registered Representative's "Top 100," September 1, 2009 bases its rankings exclusively on quantitative criteria: assets under management, size of the book, and an acceptable compliance record. Nominations are not accepted. The rating is not indicative of the Financial Advisor's future performance. Morgan Stanley Smith Barney does not pay a fee to Registered Representative in exchange for the rating.

Whoops...

It occurred to me that I never said a word about my private life.

Here goes a bit, but not too much.

I strive to be a community leader. For example, I'm a member of the Board of Trustees for The Guardian Angels. I was awarded the "Cyberangel of the Year Internet Safety Award," which was presented to me by Former New York City Mayor, Michael Bloomberg at the Angel's annual Gala event. I received a Partner in Education acknowledgment from the Mentoring Program of the New York City public school system. I am a Board Member of DoughMain, a non-profit dedicated to teaching financial literacy to children; and I am heavily involved with the Police Athletic League. I also volunteer my time coaching youth sports. I have my own team at home too—my wife, Eve, and our children, Jenna, Danny and Nick.

Keeping Kids Safe

Why is my background important to my clients? Because their backgrounds are important to me. I can understand their personal logic if I can understand who they are.

I cannot create stability for you in your portfolio if I cannot understand what derails you. I want you to have more than wealth. I want you to have peace of mind. I guarantee that money alone does not buy that.

Even The Bite can Bite You

In *Logical Investing,* I warned you to expect the unexpected even if you have a perfectly balanced and researched portfolio with lots of legitimate Bite. Why?

Because my partner is Wayne Chrebet, a famous sports figure, I cannot resist sports analogies. In writing this Chapter, Wayne and I were talking; and I asked him how, from the world of sports, he would describe preparation for the unexpected.

I knew that Wayne would come through with a highly aggressive example. Not surprisingly for a sports giant, Wayne enjoys working with individuals who have a similar competitiveness and drive. These individuals are typically highly successful, ultra-driven business owners. They exhibit the same traits that made Wayne successful in the National Football League: loyalty, the desire to compete at the highest level and to leave nothing on the table at the end of the day.

Before Wayne and I worked as a team, Wayne played with the New York Jets for 11 seasons. During his tenure with the Jets, he set the NFL record for the most receptions by a wide receiver in his first two seasons. In 2000, Sports Illustrated dubbed Wayne's career history as "one of the greatest rags to riches stories in the history of professional sports."

Wayne has received numerous awards, including New York Newsday's "Jet of the Year," the Dennis Byrd Award for "Most Inspirational Player," the New York Jets "Unsung Hero" Award, the Thurman Munson Award for outstanding efforts on and off the field and in serving the community and the Ed Block Courage Award. He has been involved with The Colleen Giblin Foundation, The United Way, The Boomer Esiason Foundation, The Starlight Foundation and the Make-A-Wish Foundation.

Wayne's eleven-year NFL career ended on a first down conversion. He went across the middle, caught the ball and got knocked out cold! He held onto that ball. It was a play that defined his career and personality. I saw it again in 2014. The NY Jets immortalized him by putting him into the Jet's *Ring of Honor*. Wayne has the biggest heart of anyone I know by a mile.

Needless to say, Wayne understands the particular type of hard-driving business person we often get as a client in our Group. He works with many of the advanced planning issues that you will read about in Chapter 22.

Wayne received an Excellence Award for his exceptional performance. He holds his Series 7 (General Securities Representative), Series 66 (State Law & Registered Investment Advisor), and Series 31 (Futures Managed Funds) licenses. He resides in Colts Neck, NJ, with his wife, Amy, and three children.

In crafting his example of how to be prepared for uncertain times, Wayne explained that coaches look at tendencies. "Some players," he said, "tend to run left when others run right. What happens when one player makes a play? We study the game plan; and when we have it tight in our mind, we can make instant changes without much thought. Yet, the decisions are right.

For example, say we are playing and the rain is torrential.

The game will never be called. We know that we will run with the ball more than we will pass because we want to avoid the winds. We know how to adjust for uncertainty and deviate from the tendency, but only because we have the typical scenario firmly in our understanding, but also we understand the dynamics of the abnormal."

When I thanked Wayne for his analogy, he wanted to add one more thing for you, the reader, to consider. He said, "You know, most great sports players end with little money. They do not rehearse for retiring from the sport."

"Why is that?" I asked, knowing that they must have many friends in the same boat that could have the experience to help them avoid such money trouble.

"Because," explained Wayne, "They think they are going to play forever. They rely on people who do not understand what is going on. They cannot see into the long-term future. They are young and indestructible, and have a Superman complex."

In this respect they, and we, all create The Fluff of our lives. We paint that pretty picture. We believe our own Bark, our own wishes and self-stories that we hope will fuel us on our journey to achieve. Without them. I could never be a success after emigrating from Russia, and Wayne would not be wearing that Jets Ring of Honor ring.

At the New York Stock Exchange Celebrating Wayne's Induction into the NY Jets "Ring of Honor"

Chapter 4

The Bite of Dispassion

"As has been stated, the innate false appearance of speculative surroundings does much to influence public participation at the wrong period. When stocks are low in price the brokerage offices are deserted, the newspapers say little of speculative affairs, transactions are limited, and those who have been worsted in the preceding declines speak in pessimistic terms of the future. A long period of dullness almost invariably follows a severe decline, new lambs must be born and the old ones suffered to grow a new fleece, and dullness is always unattractive. But at the crest of a great movement all is activity. Excited groups gather about the tickers and predict future events found principally on illusions or hope, and stories of quickly acquired gains are heard on every hand."

The Pitfalls of Speculation, by Thomas Gibson, The Moody Corporation, 1906

While we would like to think that we rationally approach moneymaking with an eye toward investing with the right risk/reward ratio, sadly that is not true.

Even in visiting a financial planner, there remains that spark of hope that he or she will do a card trick that gets quick results overnight.

For some, the wishful thinking is quite the opposite. Instead of hoping for an overnight windfall and taking too many chances, they opt for a head-in-the-sand approach. That sort of investor often does nothing until prices rise with his or her comfort zone along with it. Hence, the usual problem of "buy high sell low" raises its head again.

Even the best investors with good solid portfolios have diminished investor returns of as much is 3% per year because of their psychological bent to get in when everyone else does and get out when everyone else does.

One real-life client example was a gentleman who never touched his 401k over a five-year period. Against my advice, he put the majority of his qualified portfolio into technology/internet funds. He got lucky with an extended tech bull market. But, he learned the wrong lesson. Buy and hold is not always the best way when you own a narrow sector, or are over-concentrated in one sector. When the dotcom bubble collapsed, so did he.

So whether you are in danger of a 'set it and forget it' philosophy or a 'run with the herd' tinkering bend, you diminish your bottom line.

To do well and not run with the herd, we need to feel a sense of mastery and comfort.

And here is where the real danger lies. Advisors can easily play into these emotions without ever breaking the law or running afoul of compliance. They simply make you feel comfortable about wrong choices. And so investors are doubly challenged. First, to eschew their own emotional inadvertent misleading behavior and thought process and, second, to not fall prey to the feel good advisor who is often a long-time friend or colleague?

In the long run, steady, calculated investing infused by the knowledge of a professional research team will win the day.

It is not that we are unaware of what we are doing. We know very well when we fear to invest, when we take a flyer because we got a tip, or when we simply do not pay attention.

Very few of my clients commit the sin of staying out of the market and keeping large sums of cash. Nevertheless, in a virtually zero interest rate environment, I am shocked at how many are still keeping an overly dangerous amount in cash.

Yes, I said dangerous. Under very few circumstances has cash outperformed even a moderately diversified portfolio over time.

And today, although at the moment the dollar is strong, our national debt does not portend well for holding cash. Why? With the high debt policy of our government, our dollar could become deflated. If the Yuan becomes a reserve currency, the dollar could also lose out as the world's first commercial currency.

When the dollar is deflated, you may have money; but you do not have buying power.

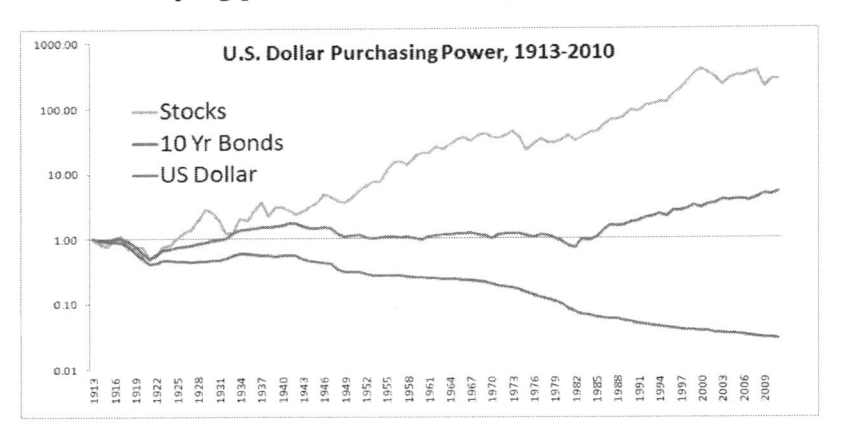

U.S. Dollar Purchasing Power, 1913-2010
— Stocks
— 10 Yr Bonds
— US Dollar

A client of mine made an excited phone call to me recently. She had discovered a windfall. She received a letter in the mail from a retrieval company that told her she had an abandoned account. In the end, the windfall equaled $180,000. The initial investment was $15,000.

It was clear to me that the best thing that ever happened with this investment was that it had been forgotten and allowed to grow. I can guarantee you that my client would have either spent the money or cashed out for a more secure investment, even though it fit perfectly into the original allocation.

There are hundreds of examples, probably many in your life when we simply make a mistake. And I do not mean simply investment mistakes. Also, mistakes about whom you trusted with your money, the way you handled your money, whom you allowed to influence your decision making, and ultimately your returns.

It would be nice to simply say "trust me."

I will be brash. In most cases I make money for people. In many cases, I would make even more if they stayed out of it. But, through the years, I have discovered that they do not like that much and neither do I.

So, what can we do about it?

True, there are formulaic ways of approaching even our emotions. I do like to have clients assessed by my team to see what their financial personality really is. There are many clues.

Some of which include:

- How you have invested in the past
- Your level of wealth
- Your core decision makers and major influencers
- If you are in business, your management style

But, nothing is more telling than what you tell me. What is your risk tolerance, does it differ from your co-decision makers? What keeps you up at night?

Any financial plan must begin with a willingness to invest in the first place.

For those who have high anxiety around investing, that will not happen until the media, a high S&P, and a brother-in-law bragging about his portfolio, there is a perfect storm that pushes them over the edge to take a position. So overcoming this reluctance is important. But, it is also where the big talkers, the smooth operators, can come in and create a zone of comfort for you that are really not matched by the wisdom of their investments.

Then there are the tinkerers and those who constantly have buyer's remorse.

Unable to stick with a decision, ever meddling in his own financial future, uncomfortable with the choices he has made, he trades constantly, usually in the wrong direction.

While it is easy to see how we might stay out of the market through fear or pay a high price for our exuberance, it is more puzzling as to why we might let a bad decision ride into the ground. In fact, these mistakes are all dictated by the same brain function. We just do not want to take a loss.

The amygdala, the part of the brain that we call "fight or flight" is the most primitive and least rational part of our brain. It is there for one purpose: self-protection, perhaps the strongest urge known to mankind. If there is any chance of danger, the amygdale kicks in.

When it tells us not to do something, to not invest, we fight the instinct to make money.

The instinct not to lose money wins in a heartbeat. We often take flight with the help of the amygdale.

One of the first books to acknowledge this was *Money Think*, by Adriane Berg, Pilgrim Press.

Since that early work, there have been devised many sophisticated, quantitative tests to understand your personal psychology so that your portfolio is NOT tanked by your behavior.

I like any sort of introspection that gets you further in touch with yourself and allows me as your advisor to work through any anxiety you may have. But, to be blunt, my job is to make money for you. When I do that your anxiety is low. If it does not happen, your anxiety is high. And all of the behavioral psychology issues kick in because of your reaction to results.

I believe that results, and only results, are The Bite.

Those with theories, fancy charts and hot tips can Bark all they want. The media and the stories they tell can add some amusing Fluff, but that is not what I am after.

I am surrounded by a team of the most competent, kind and emotionally intelligent people. It is a good thing, too. I concentrate on The Bite. I want to make sure you will hold a winning hand, and I cannot do that by handholding.

I pride myself on having incredibly close relationships with many of my clients. I worked with them on their charities, we hang out. But, these relationships with some of the brightest executives and business owners in the world come from the fact that they can rely on my rock steady ability to focus on results.

Most of my clients, oh heck, all of my clients are wealthy by any comparative standard. Most of them, like me, got that way on their own. Astronauts, sports figures, moguls of industry and corporate executives have some or all of their investments managed by my team.

I understand that all of your emotional triggers, fear, greed, reluctance, pride, trust and past experience will color the way you read what I write. That is as it should be. But, I hope you will come away from these words with a better understanding of how to focus on The Bite and ignore The Bark and The Fluff.

Chapter 5

The Bite of Knowledge

"Every affair of life is preceded by certain signs, and coming events cast their shadows before in the stock market as well as in other affairs."

The Pitfalls of Speculation, by Thomas Gibson, The Moody Corporation, 1906

Let me give you a hint of how we use logic* to benefit our clients. First, we really get to know them. Next, we think about them and their needs, not just when we are making trades or shifting their allocations.

*I have included material on the academics of logic in Appendix III. If you truly get interested in how logic can change your way of thinking, perhaps in more than just money management, you can take a free course on logic at: http://philosophy.hku.hk/think/logic/whatislogic.php.

A logical approach to personal finance must be holistic, since logic does not flourish in a vacuum.

It needs to be guided by experts. I would have insufficient knowledge of the buying environment if not for my Wealth Management team members. It is logical for me to surround myself with the best in very different narrow skills rather than the jacks-of-all-trades.

Particularly when our clients own a business, we need to plan for its sale and position it for tax savings several years before they have any intent to sell. We need to consider management succession, looking at alternatives for family transfers and employee compensation.

Yet, these essentials of logical thought often elude advisors.

Here is our protocol:

- Know the client.
- Know the totality of their financial picture.
- Arrange things to care for all their financial needs.
- Use true experts to identify problems and opportunities the client cannot see for themselves.

When our team applies logic to preserve and grow our clients' wealth, we do not stop with investment decisions or portfolio management.

Our planning encompasses other topics, including the following:

- Estate planning
- Tax planning
- Business succession
- Inheritance and family values
- Successful aging
- Home ownership
- Education costs
- Special events and celebrations
- Business selling and evaluation

We look at all these as well as many other aspects of our clients' financial life that could use an infusion of logic.

To know what they are, we have to know you.

Rate from one to ten the importance to you of each of the below issues, and write down how long they have been on your mind and unresolved. Then prioritize which decisions have been lingering.

What Is Stopping You From Taking Action?

	Importance	Length of Decision Period	What's Stopping You?
	(1-10)	(6 mos, 1,2,3, years, 3+ years)	
It's About Money			
Selling Your Business			
Lifelong Financial Independence			
Refinancing a Business/Real Estate			
Tax Issues			
Leaving a Legacy			
It's About Family			
Aging Parents			
Grandchildren			
Boomerang Children			
Marriage and Divorce			
It's About Lifestyle			
Where to Live			
Where to Retire			
How to Follow Passionate Life Purpose			
Philanthropy			

Take the decision that is highest on the list and has waited the longest, and tackle that first.

Determine why you have not made the decision.

Here are the top three possibilities:

- Too complex: Should I sell my home?
- Not enough information: How do I get the best college loan?
- Emotional: Shall I sell a stock that has tanked and take a loss?

Sometimes we discover that the obstacle in making decisions is a combination of emotions and the need for practical advice. In that case, I can often solve the problem through solid research. Here is where true knowledge can replace fears and get us moving. Often a client's issues are resolved through accurate research and the guidance of experts.

For example, a tax question, an issue of currency exchange, only takes expertise. A question of the fate of a company or its creditworthiness, the health of a fund manager, takes the input of people who have a constant eye on a situation.

We seek asset allocation guidance from experts.

We consider the economic views of David Malpass, Larry Kudlow, CNBC, David Darst of Morgan Stanley Smith Barney, and Barry Habib a foremost authority on rates for the mortgage industry, Chief Market Strategist at MBS Highway and Hans Olsen who sat 30 feet away from me in my last office. We use Bloomberg Research. I also get research and advice from Nick Ponzio, former head of Hill Thompson, which was later bought by Dain Raucher and the Royal Bank of Canada. Nick is a friend and the best trader I have ever seen. These are only a few of our resources.

There is no question that EXPERT analysis creates a comfort zone that makes rational decisions possible and takes us off the dime.

What I am most proud of is making my clients' lives simpler; they know the investing parameters without suffering over the decisions. I know them, and I am thinking on their behalf.

That is why I use mind mapping to really understand their issues and their worlds.

Mind Mapping: I am part psychologist, part financial advisor and part investment manager.

Once you get the answers to the many intake questions your advisor poses, what will the typical financial advisor do with them? I cannot speak for others, but what we at The Moldaver Group do is *mind mapping*. We take your financial life and make it into a flow chart.

This is a depth level that allows us to make those holistic decisions that are eluding you. We pride ourselves in just beginning where other advisors leave off.

Your values, goals, relationships, assets, advisors, process and interests.

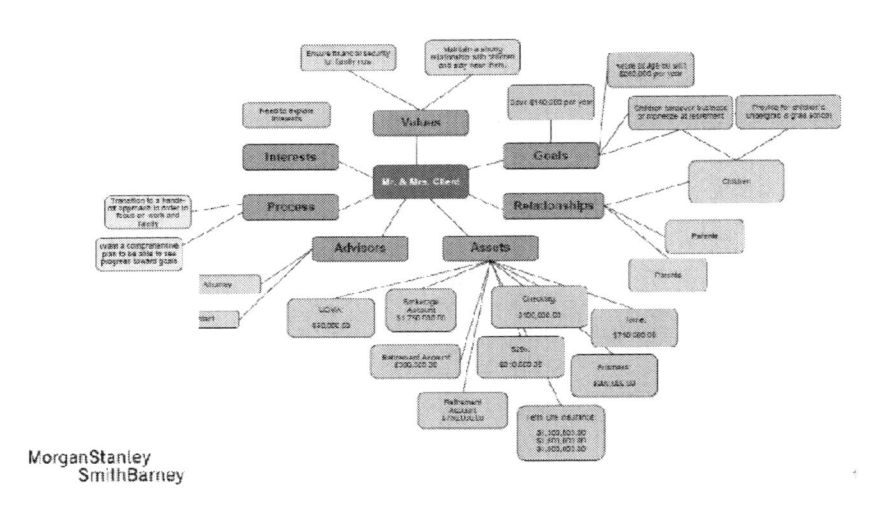

MorganStanley
SmithBarney

Here is what a complete mind map looks like, but do not be alarmed at the detail. Most of us just need to concentrate on one or two areas. In this situation, a financial planning group like ours, with separate in-depth expertise, really comes in handy. We can do complete planning for you.

This is the ultimate in logical investing. Know who you are first, and the money will follow.

That is why we ask you nearly 100 questions about yourself and do not get to a question on your money until question number 60!

This is What I Stare At All Day

Page 73

Chapter 6

The Bite of Experience

Thinking outside the box is hard when our habits keep barking at us.

Because of the changes in domestic and global economies, most of my clients are on unfamiliar turf. Their old habits are no longer working for them. If they made a mistake in the past volatile years, they are often paralyzed to make a move, as new habits are hard to acquire in stressful times.

The traditional avenues of conservative investing are no longer available. There is no place to retreat. Yet, some income investments still pay 6-7%, but require a long-term lock-in, disregarding what happens if rates rise. We analyze whether the need for current income trumps the need for future price protection.

We have seen in the previous Chapters that as the selection of assets become more complex and the markets are more correlated because of globalization, the simple idea that stocks will balance out bonds has less validity.

We need to cultivate new habits to make decisions in a world with different fundamentals.

Turn your habit box into a breakthrough triangle:

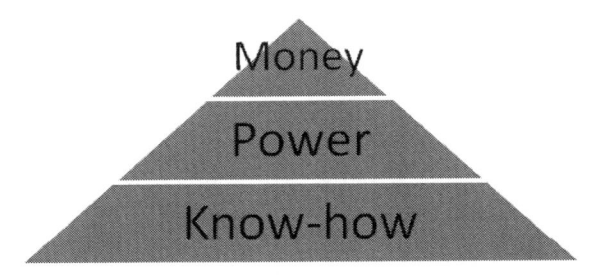

```
        Money
       Power
      Know-how
```

Know-how: My favorite example of logical planning through know-how parallels the great strategic alliance triangle of know-how, power and money.

A client came to me wanting to refinance 19 properties and was concerned over the 19 closing costs he would encounter. He asked if I knew anyone that could make closing more cost-effective. The closing costs alone would have been $100,000 or more.

I thought about it logically and came to the conclusion that his portfolio of bonds could be borrowed against with no closing costs and at a lower rate than was being offered by mortgage companies. Also, there would be virtually no paperwork.

He could never have seen this solution on his own; he did not have the know-how. Even if he had the understanding, he still needed a firm with the power and caring to make it happen for him.

Yes, he had the money. That is the client's contribution to the triangle. But, with a powerful, full-service Wealth Manager like The Moldaver Group, with high level know-how, the job gets done by thinking outside the box.

Please do not think I am arrogant about our Group. I am proud. It is important to consider that we are much more than brokers for our clients; we are wealth managers. That means from taxes to trusts, business valuation to college planning, it is the techniques and alternative options we can reveal to you and help implement that increase our value to you.

One reason people cannot think outside the box is lack of knowledge or familiarity with what is available to them. We are your breakout guides.

Experience:

Outside-the-box thinking is not always about smart strategies. It is often about the fundaments of investing itself.

Here is another example from a real-life client whose habit almost ruined him financially. Mr. X had a municipal bond portfolio that he had bought for safety. It had painfully dropped some 15% or 20% in 90 days. Mr. X did not succumb to his "sell low" panic habit.

This was remarkable because he was not alone in panicking. Many people were stunned as their advisors had never prepared them for the market fluctuations associated with even high-grade bonds if interest rates rose. Remember, over the last 20 years we had a bull market in bonds and saw the 10 year Treasury yield fall from double digits to 1.5%. However, when borrowing ceased after the Lehman collapse and yields on corporate bonds rose dramatically, the picture was not pretty.

Clients freaked out. Many took flight to gold and treasuries. But, we had already put Mr. X in assets that moved in the opposite direction of bonds, so his portfolio was in balance.

I do not want this to sound easy. We labor long and hard to get the right balance through multi-asset class and diversified asset allocation.

Many advisors and even fund managers call their strategies "asset allocation," and they think that just having an asset mix is enough. It may have been at one time when economist Harry Markowitz won the Nobel Prize for his theory that asset classes are more important than selecting the right individual investment or stock. But, things are more complex now, as we have seen.

Habitually conservative investors will not see the need for stocks. Risk-takers may feel lower interest rate secured bonds are a waste of growth opportunity. So, the former struggle with low return portfolios and the latter take risks that can wipe them out.

We see it and guide you.

Once you have lived through a balancing success, like our bond client, you start to think outside the box and stop habitual investing.

Business Success Syndrome

We call another "habit" some of our clients display Business Success Syndrome. They get so caught up in the value of their business or in the running of it that they do not plan for liquidity down the line or have no exit plan when they decide to sell. They have not maximized benefits in such a way as to really incentivize their employees for greater loyalty and productivity. It is hard to see that investing is also an HR issue. We see the total picture and can think outside the box for them.

The "Warren Buffett Syndrome"

When it comes to thinking outside the box and changing habits, one behavior I think we need to quash is "mimicking." We love gurus, and Mr. Buffett certainly is one. But in 2008, his portfolio was off 35%. That is way too much risk for many of my clients. It would go against the "stress test" we have already discussed and which you will read about again later. Everyone wants Buffet's performance, but not all are prepared for his volatility and underperformance in certain periods.

If I could have everyone think outside their box in just one area, it would be to arrive at the "Rate of Return" (how much money they need their money to make) to reach their financial goal.

living living living living

Monmouth County's Luxury Magazine Network

THE JERSEY SHORE · COLTS NECK · HOLMDEL · MARLBORO

Early Holiday 2008 - November

Our Pick:

Edward Moldaver

Wealth Manage & Advisor

One thing is for sure...the market is definitely volatile. More than ever it is important to work with a financial advisor who is on top of his game. Meet Edward Moldaver, a Senior Vice President with Morgan Stanley in Red Bank. Moldaver recently joined the company after leaving Bear Stearns, where he was a Senior Managing Director. He is one of the top wealth management advisors in the country and sees to it that he is well versed in what's going on in the world around us each and every day, which helps him make the best decisions with your money.

Moldaver says, "Every one of my clients is on a specific plan. We plan for times like these. For more than the 200 years that this country has been around, the United States of America has had a 100% success rate in overcoming every obstacle that we have encountered."

This Colts Neck resident, who has about 20 years of experience, runs a wealth management team of five people, most of whom also made the move from Bear Stearns. By working with The Moldaver Group you'll reap many benefits, including: a completely customized approach and a unique written plan; detailed and consolidated records of your assets and account activity; access to market-leading research; and IPO's. The managers here are experienced in managing wealth for high-net-worth individuals and corporations.

In addition to putting together the best portfolio for your needs while backing the Morgan Stanley platform, Moldaver says, "Our group works with our client's attorneys to ensure the best care when it comes to creating trusts and estate plans, as well."

Put your trust in this team and call their toll-free number [(800) 418-8352] to schedule an appointment. For further information about Morgan Stanley, please refer to the website.

-by Gayle Davis

In this article, dated 2008, I went on the record as saying that I believe in investing in the USA. The US overcomes its obstacles and market turmoil 100% of the time and remains the oldest extant republic in history. When we have a financial obstacle, we overcome it too by betting on America.

Page 78

Part II

There is an "I" in Bite and an "I" in Team

Chapter 7

Building a Wealth Management Infrastructure with Bite

The decision-making process is as important as the decision itself because the right process precedes a good decision. You are about to get an ear full of how we do things to create your decision-making infrastructure.

Whatever the nature of the decision you must make, whether about money or anything else, it is most logical to have a process or infrastructure for making your decision. That is why we spend so much time in crafting the process that works for you.

You will not be surprised to learn that part of the structure is determining who else needs to make decisions with you.

Of course, most of the time husbands and wives make decisions together. But, lately, we have also discovered that parents and children, and even grandchildren, make intergenerational decisions, particularly when adult children are caring for elderly parents.

Determine how much time, effort and input you want in the decision-making process.

We also focus on how much you want to be involved in the day-to-day decision making.

- How many face-to-face meetings do you want a year?

- How often do you want to have updates on your portfolio?
- Do you want a call when there is a change in the market, even if we have discretion over your account?
- Do you want email communications?
- How confidential do you want your file? Do you want us to share it with other advisors, i.e., attorneys and your tax professional?

Before you meet with us at our office, or make any financial plan, realize that it is an ongoing process. Think about some of these things, so that the entire decision-making infrastructure can be held together by what's important to you.

Know your core values.

While we are talking about YOU, let us not discount your values. We dig deep into what you are interested in for yourself, for your family, and for the world. When we ask you to identify your "core values," we really pay attention, because the value section of your "life file" is part of the infrastructure that guides us in making a financial decision.

In an earlier chapter, I mentioned my studies at Wharton. Here is a perfect quote from the materials that were part of my instruction. It expresses exactly why we create an infrastructure AND a consultative atmosphere.

Our goals are "trust, growing the relationship and delighting the client ... delivering a consistent, high-quality client experience will enable you to easily differentiate yourself from your competition."

Put another way, we want you to rely on us, and you could never do that if you didn't realize that we are on your side. We begin with the discovery meeting to uncover your important financial issues, life goals and collect information. Our clients are busy, and so we do what is necessary to prepare for the meeting and make it efficient. In fact, you will find some of that preparation in the Appendices of this book.

Set up a scalable protocol.

After the discovery meeting, we can move on to an investment planning meeting. This can take place in the next week or the next day, depending on your time frame. If you are ready to create a discretionary account with us, we are ready for you in every case. About six weeks later, we have a follow-up meeting. All your account paperwork is organized, and we set up a structure for our continuous communication. We engage **with you** in regular contact meetings, depending on your time frame.

If all this client-centric activity is not happening for you now, with your advisors, you have not set up a winning infrastructure for decision making.

Diversification

Even when we have full discretion over our client's accounts, we map out a risk-based asset allocation model they approve of and understand. We make portfolio changes pretty strictly within the decision-making criteria that we map out. Of course, we have quarterly meetings at the very least, so that if the risk allocation changes because of something in your life or thinking, we can readjust our model.

We do have certain parameters, though. If a client is somewhat optimistic about the stock market and able to take more risk, we might map out an allocation of 50% in stock and 50% in bonds or other income producers. Our parameter may be optimistic enough to go 55% stocks, but never above. If pessimistic, 30%, but never below.

By contrast, for a very conservative investor with a low-risk tolerance, we might map out a 15-25% range. It's not cookie cutter or a fixed percentage for everyone, just a way of restoring balance in the context of the client's temperament.

Of course, this is very simplified, as we have the world of investment choice at our fingertips. But truth be told, the major sectors of portfolio allocation make for a large percentage of your success.

Asset allocation is of greater importance to your success than the investments you choose in each class, this Modern Portfolio Theory won a Noble Prize in Economics.

- Equity/income balance: The balance between equity (ownership in a company), and lending to a company or government bonds is not the only criteria we map out. Within each of these asset classes, we have additional categories. For example, within the stock category, we would look at value stocks, small-cap stocks, large growth stocks, international stocks and create an allocation that we find reasonable for making decisions about a particular client.

- Investment managers that outperform the market: We believe that because of excellent research and experience, some people, like ourselves and other money managers with whom we work, are better at picking investments and outperforming the market as a whole. So, we select managers that are very knowledgeable about one particular area of investing. A good example is the well-known author and money manager, James P. O'Shaughnessy. I highly recommend that you read his national bestseller, *What Works on Wall Street*. I also recommend that you read his Preface to this book if you have not already done so.

This is much more satisfactory than a plain vanilla allocation. There is nothing wrong with that either; in fact, many clients with smaller accounts need to use Exchange Traded Funds (ETFs), to get the allocations that will serve to diversify their portfolio, without having to buy 100 shares of stock or more, in just one company.

As I have stated before, we are more than money managers or investment advisors. We are financial advisors. So, we also work with an eldercare specialist. When our clients need specialized decision making for healthcare, legal documents or even a home renovation for successful aging, we have a specialist that can help you make those decisions as well.

Use specialists.

When we look for a specialist in investing or in advanced planning to help make decisions with us, we look for certain characteristics.

They are:

- What is their process? How do they make decisions?

- Can their past successes be duplicated in good economic times and in bad economic times?

- What are the characteristics with which they deliver performance, more or less volatility than their benchmark?

Many advisors simply look at an investment advisor's *last* 3 to 5 years of performance.

We actually want to "psych out" or predict the ***next*** 3 to 5 years of performance. To do that, we look at the way a money or fund manager makes a decision, how consistently right or wrong they have been and under what circumstances. Can they duplicate their process in the future?

The emphasis we put on the profile, policy and investment style of a money manager is extraordinary. To me, it is the hidden secret of success in investing. Even the very wealthy use funds, hedge funds, REITs to diversify sufficiently. Experts must select the contents of these funds. I have repeated to my team, and I suggest to you, that the people running the funds, selecting the managers and the culture of the professionals at the fund is of utmost importance. Who got divorced? Is ill? Is dissatisfied with compensation?

If anyone refuses to believe there are human beings behind the choices, they cannot outperform the market indices. Neither luck, magic, bite nor fluff outperform the market. Only people can.

The Moldaver Group Team Specialists

We have many members of our team and growing. Let me introduce just two of them to give you a flavor of the variety of skills and personalities we bring to the table.

A Word from Wayne Chrebet

By now you know that I played in the NFL before forming my partnership with Ed Moldaver. Because I humbly acknowledge that I had a famous career in sports, you might be curious as to why I chose financial advising as my second career, and why I chose to work with Ed Moldaver, in particular.

Let me explain.

Sports, football in particular, can be a short-lived career. I retired at age 31. I admit that I was bewildered and could have gone in many directions. Many people assume that when you retire from a lucrative, demanding and rewarding career, the rest is gravy. I know full well that is certainly not the case.

Whether it's the NFL, an executive corporate position or business you build yourself, there is a highly emotional side to success and to being emotionally ready to take the next step, particularly when you retire at a young age.

Ed's clients were not only successful, they were also what I might call 'precocious.' Many had the means to be financially ready to retire way before the usual age 65; many before age 40. I was drawn to that and hoped that I could help people in that position as I had once needed help myself. For example, I stayed on my own financially. Most of my colleagues ignored financial planning. They were making a great deal of money; but, finances, math, figures and all that went with it were not in their comfort zone.

None of them had a play by play for their financial life. This is something anyone needs who retires at an early age. Perhaps even more than those who retire in their 50s, 60s and 70s, you must have a plan of what you will do with your life; and you must be able to fund it for very many decades.

There's more to it than even that. I have received The Ring of Honor. For some people, I am a role model. Many successful people in business are also role models. They retire with money. Now what?

This crossroads must be understood emotionally and structured properly by a financial advisor. For many people, it sounds like a good problem. There are opportunities to do things for the world, for your community, for your family, and for yourself that are unprecedented unless you take the wrong turns.

Unfortunately, it's very easy to go wrong; but not with my guidance. I'm absolutely committed that people take the right direction so that things don't go wrong the way they do with many sports figures and business folks as well.

This isn't really surprising. Frankly, in my experience with Ed, most of our clients are self-made, as are Ed and I. Very few were trust fund babies or born with silver spoons. Actually, as our clients get older, we are meeting with wealthy inheritors, their children. They may have the same emotional financial issues even younger in life than sports figures and high-level entrepreneurs.

As for me, I was the child of middle-class parents with an honestly very happy youth. Whenever we could, we went to the backyard and played ball. I simply loved to catch and throw. From the minute I experienced football, that's all I really wanted to do in life.

Some of my fans acknowledge that I am not a big guy physically compared to the others who played my same position in the great sport of football. So, they wonder, how did it happen that I could excel in this sport of giants? I credit my parents who taught me to never give up. I know it sounds like a cliché and something you just say for the press. But, for me, it's true.

Let's just say I'm like a dog with a bone. I'm just not going to let go.

And that came to money too! My first big paycheck came with my first contract when I was 21 years old. I remember to the penny how much I earned, $119,000. Today young newbies playing my same position start out with $425,000. But, for me, my $119.000 was just a ton of money.

I had no advisors. My middle-class parents did not know what to do with that kind of income. I was one of the too few sports figures that actually went to a financial planner from the very beginning. Even as a young man, I enjoyed working side-by-side with my advisor and seeing what he was doing. But, I certainly did not expect to be a financial advisor myself.

Eventually, it was time for me to graciously leave the sport that I loved. I was bewildered as to where my life would take me. It was then that I met Ed. He got the idea that we could do great things together. If you know Ed, then you know that very few people can say 'no' to him because he always makes so much sense. I was inspired to work with him and have done so for the past seven years to great success.

Of course, many of the clients I bring to our financial team are sports figures. People wonder how with such high salaries, it's possible for many of them to end up with very little money and even go into bankruptcy. Here's where I come in because I understand how this can happen. Let me explain and also tell you why my experience with sports figures is relevant to you.

First, sports careers are not only often short-lived, but sometimes come to an abrupt and unanticipated end. As a result, I'm always looking for the exit plan and the endgame for all of my clients. The entrepreneur who eventually wants to stop working 24/7 or start something new also needs to be financially independent.

Second, as soon as a sports figure begins to make good money, friends and extended family start asking for financial help. I know because it happened to me. We get inundated, and we feel guilty about saying 'no.' Because our clients are very wealthy, the same thing happens to them. Sometimes I have to be the coach to make sure they say 'no' in the right way and say 'yes' in the right way, as well.

Third, everybody brings you a deal. Does that sound familiar? Sports figures are brought most real estate, restaurant, automobile dealership and auto repair deals. The one thing they all have in common is that they are a 'sure thing.' Invest in enough sure things and you'll go broke. It's our job to investigate each and every single deal that clients bring to us to vet for them. We take nothing for granted.

Please read the piece later on in the book by Peter Grupe, a retired FBI Executive Manager with over 30 years' experience in law enforcement and corporate finance, formerly responsible for managing the White Collar Crime Branch of the New York office of the FBI. He is at our disposal to vet people and deals as he analyzes risks for our clients.

Finally, the way I met Ed was through charities. He's very philanthropic, and so am I. We are both very fond of working with people who have built their own wealth and are philanthropic, as well. We also know that not all charities are legitimate and need to be checked out. We know there are ways of maximizing the good we do in the world. We help our clients with all of this.

People asked me whether I miss playing football. Of course, I do. But, in the long run, I would not trade the team that I am on now for anything. Because I was a player my whole life, I like being part of a team. I probably could have put out a shingle of my own. I would never do that, particularly as soon as I met Ed. It is my privilege to serve you and to work with him.

Another significant member of our Group is Assistant Vice President, Mary Sliwa, whom we call 'the glue' that binds our clients and the advisors. Mary understands the importance and value of earning trust.

With over 25 years' of experience as an executive in media, fundraising, philanthropy and management, Mary draws on her diverse background to enhance her clients' financial objectives. Her holistic focus is on managing our clients' relationships with integrity, competency and accessibility. Mary's love of coalition building has provided her with deep knowledge of the complex issues surrounding philanthropy and endowment that affect high net worth clients.

Mary coordinates The Moldaver Group's strategic relationships through her vast personal and business networks of executives, philanthropists, public servants and media figures. As the female voice in the Group, Mary is cognizant of the unique issues facing female clients and couples is mindful of the realities of home-life, relationships, and transitions; and can guide clients who desire to leave behind a legacy.

For over 13 years, Mary was the Chief Operating Officer and Executive Director of The Guardian Angels, a volunteer-based organization made up of dedicated individuals who donate their time and energy to help protect communities around the world. Mary led the Angels' evolution from well-known New York City grassroots street patrols to a respected community safety organization on a global stage. In this role, Mary developed the organization's board of directors; overseeing all marketing, advertising and public relations efforts; spearheading all fundraising including marquee gala events. Through her efforts, The Guardian Angels won recognition from major political and governmental agencies, including the awarding of the "Keys to the City" by New York City Mayor Michael Bloomberg, the Liberty Medal Award, and the President's Service Award, presented in 1998 by President Clinton for the organization's *CyberAngels* Internet safety program.

Earlier in her career, Mary had distinguished herself as a leading executive in the corporate media arena. She managed advertising sales, client relations and marketing programs for Capital Cities/WABC Radio and was awarded the company's prestigious "Circle of Excellence" honor. She also held executive positions at CNN/Headline News and radio outlets WPAT, WPLJ, and WRKS, and lectured at New York University.

A Word from Mary Sliwa

I want to share with you the strength I personally feel in working as a partner in The Moldaver Group. I believe that confidence in an advisor is built when our clients know that our first priority is to address their individual needs and they know they are listened to and heard.

There is value in having similar experiences as our clients. I've learned from going through some of the many life transitions that both men and women go through- divorce, retirement, death of a spouse, birth of a child, caring for an elderly parent, re-marriage, donating to a philanthropic endeavor or leaving a legacy.

The Moldaver Group's idea of a "family office," is to be like a family. We're there to help our clients in many areas of their lives. We communicate with our client's accountants, insurance agencies, divorce lawyers, trusts and estates attorneys, and anyone else with whom our clients would like us to be involved with.

I met Ed through his work with several charitable organizations, and I found a leader I could trust.

Know your risk tolerance.

We also are careful to be sure that all of our advisors have different mindsets - some who believe in liquidity, some who manage alternative investments like gold and silver and other metals, some who specialize in tax-advantaged investments, and many more.

We want the benefit of many types of thinking built into our client's infrastructure. Even within the category of value domestic stock managers, you want diversity of thinking. One manager might invest in the 30 Blue Chips that comprise the Dow. One might concentrate on value ratings and balance sheets; while still another manager looks at stocks that respond to world events, like an energy stock.

This will lessen the probability of the allocation holding investments that are correlated to each other and move in lock step. With true diversity within an asset class, one of your holdings will 'zig' in price when the other 'zags.' The result is a balanced portfolio, reduced volatility and the stomach to outwait a bear market.

A good example is the use of a covered call strategy. The brilliant O'Shaughnessy does not "hedge" his stock purchases. In other words, he does not protect a portfolio if the market goes down. This is because he is truly proficient in outperforming the market, most of the time. But, for conservative clients "most of the time" is not good enough. So, for them, we might also include a money manager who sells "calls."

A "covered call" is a strategy that protects your downside. You own stock, but you sell the right of another investor to buy the stock from you at a certain price, higher than you paid. Since they pay you for that privilege, you bought a stock and also made a little income immediately. Of course, if this stock skyrockets, you have limited your profits. On the other hand, you've given a boost to your overall wealth by selling the covered call.

There are always pros and cons to any strategy. Safety might come at a long-term cost. While you achieve less volatility, you also cap your upside over time and will likely make less money in the long run.

We create our own "ecosystem."

You can see that this type of investing, plus advanced tax and legal strategies, requires a team of experts. In addition to the investing prowess we have, we also have created a system to work with attorneys in succession and estate planning, as well as tax professionals.

Wherever I have my office, I want experienced attorneys sitting nearby ready to deal with all questions. There may be ongoing changes in my client's business, net worth, or family relationships.

For the affluent client, decisions are not simple. Very often a tax problem is exasperated by even a good investment, and the net aftertax result is a loss. In my philosophy, you cannot give excellent service in an investment vacuum. Sometimes I need to act quickly and pounce on an opportunity. With other professionals at my immediate disposal, I can be sure that no problems will arise to upset a prior plan. Of course, we are happy to work with the professionals you bring to us. We have a truly holistic picture of your situation by meeting your tax and legal advisors. Unfortunately, as we meet these pros, we often discover that they have plans in their file, on the average of nine years old, because their client's financial advisor never gave them updated information. We believe the two-way flow of information, with your approval, is best.

It's important to understand that an ecosystem for our clients must have true bite. One example is our affiliation with Peter Grupe, formally with the FBI, managing over 200 operatives. Imagine finding a private opportunity that would be perfect for your portfolio offered by an unknown group and supported by calculations and assumptions that are difficult for you to evaluate. Now, imagine that you bring this opportunity to an ordinary advisor. Not only might they refuse to get involved because it is not part of their routine customer service; but, they might not know how to help you at all.

You'll never find this with our team. It is complete with the ability to analyze, evaluate, and sometimes even finance the opportunities you find on your own. That's why we make sure that we have access to the 'smarts' of a Peter Grupe, so you can gain faith and trust in him, or run the other way based on a thorough investigation that you could never have done on your own and that no attorney or accountant could help you navigate.

A Word from Peter Grupe:

Today's business world has become more and more challenging every day. The phrase "know your customer" has taken on greater meaning and significance in today's age of regulatory requirements and investor/Ponzi schemes. Large companies, investment banks and financial institutions are legally required to have sufficient knowledge of their customers and can affirmatively assert that the proceeds are not derived from criminal activity and that the principals/investors are law-abiding citizens. Terrorism financing, anti-money laundering and Ponzi schemes (Bernie Madoff, Alan Stanford) have all made the world a much more difficult place to do business since the events of September 11, 2001, and the downturn in the economy in the fall of 2008.

As a retired FBI executive in charge of white collar crime for the New York Office, and my current role as a Director with Protiviti, a global consulting firm specializing in risk and business consulting, I protect people and their assets. This is accomplished through background investigations, due diligence, forensic accounting and internal investigations. Over 30 years' of experience in the government and private sector, an international network of contacts, and access to public and proprietary data bases have enabled me to assist corporations and individuals in reducing risk. I am particularly adept at financial crimes, corruption and healthcare fraud.

There is an 'I' in TEAM.

As I have just presented, a team consists of your wealth advisors and other members, but also the 'culture' of the company in which the team functions. My clients are mainly entrepreneurs, business owners /professionals, most with type 'A' personalities. When they want something done, they expect that it happens yesterday. I suspect you know what I mean. And, so, I need an environment where I can act nimbly - where paperwork is not a burden and things happen fast.

I believe that I can get the superior investment results for clients as long as I am surrounded by my team anywhere I go. But, the process and internal culture of an organization are important to me. I suggest you take that into account also in selecting an advisor. Ask about the environment in which he or she functions. No person is an island.

And, I have strong opinions as to what does and does not work for you when it comes to a wealth management team.

Too Many Cooks, Too Little Coordination

Take the big company with 1000 to 15,000 advisors. Some of these companies have 800 offices. All the brochures say they 'specialize' in business owners. They explain their robust wealth management process and all of the moving parts are at your disposal.

The Fluff looks beautiful.

The brochures are great; but, the problem is there is no infrastructure in most of these places to actually coordinate with the economists, fixed-income and equity traders, the trust and estate advisors. Do not get me wrong, most of the bigger firms have as many brilliant people as the next; however, you, as a client, or the advisor will have virtually no contact with them. There is a difference between reading the same reports available to the entire street and having a daily conversation with a top strategist in a small forum.

There is a difference in buying bonds through a fully automated system or having an intelligent discussion with an experienced trader 30 feet away from you. There is a difference in farming out your trust and estate work to an outside attorney or having one as a partner, even right in your office. It is also useful for me to have the head of the credit department at your side to work on your lending needs with speed. An immediate, economical loan is among the greatest help we give our business-owning clients.

None of these things by themselves seem like much, but these small things, when added together, may mean the difference between 7% and 9% returns. At least, your probability of getting there will be much higher. It is important that the seven of us on our team are directly plugged into the infrastructure of the firm and that infrastructure is physically in the same location.

I like the fact that we have attorneys with 25 years' of experience or more right on our floor. Quite frankly, smaller places cannot afford this, and mega firms encourage the use of OUTSIDE 'White Glove' firms that charge the clients top dollar.

Team coordination accounts for a great deal of your financial success.

I have known very wealthy business leaders whose accountant has not spoken to their attorney in years. Of course, with Wayne Chrebet as part of my team, I think of football analogies quite frequently - nobody is quarterbacking for most business people. Entrepreneurs and top executives are so involved in growing and running their business that everything else falls by the wayside.

By the time they need help, it is too late to put a team together from scratch with all the years of background needed to make the right move.

I will give you a perfect example.

A fellow came to me selling a real estate brokerage company. He grew it from nothing. It did tremendously well, and he was selling it for hundreds of millions of dollars. He revealed to me that he was also trying to resolve some trust and estate issues. Specifically, he realized that he will end up with $100,000,000, minus taxes, in his estate. That created another problem for him when he passes. His kids will need to pay the IRS close to 50% of what is left of his estate.

He came to me two months before the sale. It was simply too late to do much. Two years prior, he could have transferred some of the stock to an irrevocable trust and at a much lower valuation.

So, who has the responsibility of knowing two years prior that this gentleman intended to sell a lucrative business? A good team would have given him a heads up that he needed to do tax planning right away before he found the buyer; if they had asked, they would have been told he was planning to sell.

I think the right team member to spot this and help him do what is best is his financial advisor. That should be the person who asks him on a regular basis what is happening in his life. How is his business going? And, then really listens to the answer. "Oh, my business is going great. We are actually up 20% over last year, and we believe the business is worth so much more."

"Is your intention to monetize that business at one point or another?"

"Sure, if I get the right number. I like to sell it in two years."

"Well, if you'd like to sell in two years, then we need to talk about potential trust and estate issues, and maybe try to get part of that business out of your estate now. We will get an evaluation that we believe will be lower right now than in two years."

There are always options. He could have done charitable planning, transfers to children, even decide whether a family limited partnership would be beneficial. The point is that by keeping a watchful eye and not just a nose to the grindstone, we see and act upon what others ignore.

Arms-length stock analysis is not current enough to make fast, accurate moves. Do not get me wrong, many brilliant strategists work at financial firms and private banks. The problem is that your advisor might never have access or interaction with them. Or, it may be very limited, like a weekly report or mass conference call.

I have always looked for and found places where my team can be nurtured by the best minds. If you ask what my strong suit is, I would say analytics and asking the right questions. I am stymied if I am not surrounded by the right people with the right answers. So, I never let that happen.

You must be humble to know what you know and what you don't know, or, at least, what others know in a specific expertise more than you.

I want to tap into their knowledge, sift their information through the funnel of my experience and apply The Bite, not The Bark or The Fluff, to your case. It is likely that the same person being interviewed on CNBC, who has the closest knowledge of a market, is also the strategist to whom I can speak directly. We have real conversations every day. In some cases, several times a day about what is happening in their investment sector.

You really cannot get any closer to the market than that. For example, when I am working with fixed-income, it is good to have access to bond traders at an institutional desk as opposed to doing everything electronically and sending your orders cross-country.

In this way, I tap into brain power at any given time instead of waiting for a specific report.

I must impress on you that even top advisors cannot, in most cases, get the analyst on the line and say, "Hey, what is going on with this stock, IPO, or what is going on with this specific closed end bond fund?"

As an investor, the importance of your advisor having close and fast access to analysts, attorneys and other specialists may seem of minimal importance. But, I know when you put it all together at the end of the year, they add up to a whole lot of performance. These individual, personal calls are my daily bread.

And, I am glad of it.

Fixed-Income Bond Trades: The Bark, The Bite, The Fluff and The Team

There are two ways of handling bond trades. One is to get to a third-party manager who selects fixed-income securities. These PROS really do get institutional and wholesale prices and charge a modest fee, generally less than 1%. Another way is looking at rates ourselves, which lamentably are at an all-time low as I write this.

Every half a percent really counts when, as now, the 10 year Treasury is at 2%. It is tough to ask somebody 1% to manage their money because that eats up most of their performance. These are very different days from the days of yore when 5%-6%-7% yields were available.

Because we have the ability to confer with a specialist, we can create a bond or fixed-income portfolio with AAA and AA rated bonds. We will not even charge an ongoing annual management fee for those (aside from a small transaction fee) even though we are selecting those bonds carefully, NOT just from 'inventory.'

Here is what I mean by The Bark when it comes to bonds. Many other firms have an inventory of their own bonds. They, of course, choose those to put in your portfolio. Such firms buy the bonds from a wholesaler, put them in their inventory and mark them up to the financial advisor.

The financial advisor picks the bonds that they like out of inventory, and puts them into your account, again with a slight markup. And, heaven help us, there may even be a management fee. By the time they get done with it, you have several extra hands in a very small pot.

Such firms know they are dealing with a captured audience. Sounds harsh, but they are basically saying, "We know you want to buy bonds. You must buy them from us." There is a difference with our team and with any advisor that I would recommend. The bonds are selected for you. Do not be fooled. Some firms will tell you with quite a Bark that they have a fixed-income trader in the group.

What they really have, and you must ask for details, is someone buying out of the firm's inventory. That is not truly having a fixed-income trader. Not when the inventory is limited.

The institutional bond traders we work with execute on behalf of financial advisors from all available bonds.

He or she is keeping an eye on everything in the market. It is a much different experience from doing business personally than electronically.

A homey analogy is a menu in a restaurant versus a personal chef. They may both have wonderful meals, but the personal chef starts from scratch, has an unlimited inventory of food from which to choose and selects from anything that would be to your taste.

The restaurant chef has a captured audience and a limited menu. Once you have selected the restaurant or the financial advisor and you decide on steak or a bond respectively, you must buy out of inventory.

I am not calling it misleading when an advisor claims they have an income securities trader on their team when all they have is an inventory selector. But, I do call it a bit of Fluff.

You might be asking yourself if you have enough money to use all these top money managers and experts.

I do not know until we really speak. It is true that some of the best investments require a big buy in. A good example is the use of hedge funds that can position themselves to buy unusual and lucrative investments. However, they often require as much as half-million dollars or more to be a participant. Individually managed sub-accounts might each request $200,000 or more per sub-account. Naturally, this helps you understand why larger investors have the potential to do better than the smaller investor. There are just some things smaller investors cannot purchase. That is where simple ETF funds can help you diversify in a specific asset class, such as real estate, international stock, emerging markets, and be in the market as a whole, which we have seen generally makes you money over the long term.

Now, let us look at why these "advantaged" investors (one's that have lots of money to invest) often DO NOT do better than the smaller investor.

Their cautionary tale will help you to avoid their mistakes and remedy your own portfolio, whatever size it might be.

Chapter 8

The Great Big Bite: Behavioral Finance

How to Match Your Temperament with Your Decisions

Years of experience have taught me that knowledge of the stock market, law, taxes, other disciplines that surround finances, and even individual wealth do not dictate investment success.

Know-how and money are just not all it takes to make the correct financial decision. It also takes a certain temperament. That is why I study the field of "behavioral finance."

Behavioral Finance is the study of how people actually behave when they gain or lose in the stock market or in any other financial endeavor. What the study of Behavioral Finance teaches will come as no surprise to you. When people gain money in any way and for any reason, they feel pride. When they lose money in the stock market or in any other way, they feel regret.

The study of Behavioral Finance helps you tap into your personal scale of pride or regret when it comes to gains or losses.

Your "financial behavioral type," will dictate how you respond to loss and gain and is influenced by many factors, including your age, your past experience, the amount of money you have accumulated, the experiences you have had with money at every stage of your life cycle.

Things have been very financially beneficial for many of us. We have crawled out of the depths created by 2008. Most of us regret not having gotten into the market sooner and many hopped in late. But, at least, we made up for some lost time.

In these better go-go times, it makes logical sense to revisit behavioral finance.

It is interesting... I can have the same client, with the same net worth with exactly the same goals; and you would think that they would have similar types of products in their financial plan.

That assumption is totally wrong. Clearly, that is because we take our clients' emotional differences, their psychological and cognitive differences into account when we suggest a portfolio.

Does that mean our work is not all about making money? No, it does not. Part of The Bite and not just The Bark is that everyone is an individual. If an investment choice does not suit you temperamentally, you will not stick with it. You will not make money from it.

For example, some people do not mind complexity. Some do. Some have beliefs that managers can outperform their index, and some believe that the markets are so efficient that one can never outperform the market consistently.

That is why some investors' asset allocation would be a plain vanilla formulaic portfolio, diversifying asset classes in a typical way, such as using Exchange Traded Funds (ETFs).

Another investor would have some fancier, more complicated choices. Both would-be winners. ETFs and index funds are all some people can tolerate without acting on fear. Others like separately managed accounts, global holdings and some exotic investments that give them greater exposure to risk. Perhaps structured products, hedge funds are within their comfort zone.

You can truly see how temperament affects money in the bad times.

When any portfolio is doing well, there is nothing wrong with any of the allocations. Everyone is happy. It is when an investment goes down in value that investors cannot understand what they own or why they bought it in the first place. Investors then make a decision based on the price and what has happened to their immediate bottom line, not the actual value or worth of what they hold.

They tend to make the wrong decision at the wrong time. To avoid this, it is actually better not to get into a good investment to begin with if it does not suit your temperament. People can reach the same goals through many different avenues. Selecting the right path is important. You will stray from the wrong path very quickly.

The path you choose should be consistent with your psychology.

If something does go wrong, you will not run away from your plan. You will stick with your decision until you achieve your goal.

Maybe I should not go there, but what comes to mind is achieving the goal of weight loss.

There are many ways to lose weight. In every case, you get exactly the same result. But, if you pick the type of diet that is unmanageable with your lifestyle, you are very likely to go off that diet and get nowhere. The next person on that diet is doing very well. It is the same diet but different people.

Similarly, with an investment you can say that you might have two people with the same weight, same body composition, and same weight loss goal, give them two completely different diets because their nutritional psychology is not the same.

Similarly, they may have very different investor portfolios because their investor psychology differs.

Let us go a little further with this same homey analogy. Take two people of the same weight who want to lose ten pounds. One is exercising, and the other one is taking weight loss drugs to suppress their appetite but is not comfortable with the plan. Now, they both get a bad cold. The one exercising stays with their program. The other one taking drugs flips out because they think the drugs may be causing a weakened immune system. This may not be the case, but they are going to act irrationally because they were never comfortable with the process.

Now, let us go back to The Bite.

Let us posit that a client bought dividend paying blue-chip stocks with a third-party manager in various sectors based on the value factors and value filters that we suggested. Historically, that manager outperformed the market 70% of the time in any one year. That leaves 30% of the time that he underperformed the market.

Because our client knew and was committed to the good value of his portfolio, he took every year of net loss in stride. Others jumped out of the growth sector only to jump back in when things were great and prices were high.

While I could explain how behavioral finance impacts investment choice in detail, I believe your best avenue to evaluating your behavioral financial style is to take the below quiz and see for yourself how you make decisions.

I also find it interesting when people make their financial decisions through a different process than they use to make their non-financial decisions. Do you?

Find out below:

Answer each question. Write your answer in the space provided. Do not do this in your head, write it down!

1. Your Decision-Making Style

- What kind of research do you do before making a decision--substantial, moderate or none?
- Do you discuss decisions with a non-professional? If so, whom?
- Where and how frequently do these discussions take place?
- Do you discuss financial decisions with a professional? If so, whom?
- Where and how frequently do these discussions take place?
- Whose opinion do you respect the most? Why?
- Whom do you trust the most to advise you?
- Are you a fast, deliberate, or slow decider?
- Once you have decided, are you quick or slow to take action?
- If slow, what usually holds you up?
- Do you carry out your decisions yourself or ask others to do so?
- Once you make a decision, how often do you change your mind? Never? Often? Sometimes?

2. Your Decision-Making History

- Give examples of times you regret having changed your mind.
- Give examples of times you are glad you changed your mind.
- Give examples of times you regret taking action.
- Give examples of times you are glad you took action.

- Analyze these. Is there a pattern in the "good" choices and actions vs. the "wrong" choices and actions?
- If so, describe the difference, i.e., did you: use different advisors for the good vs. bad decision, do more research, follow your gut instincts more, have a better understanding of the matter?

3. What Are the Ten Most Important Financial Decisions You Must Make?

Examples:

- Whether to move?
- When to retire?
- How to reinvest maturing bonds or other assets soon to become liquid?
- In whose name a gift to a child or grandchildren should be kept?
- Whether to buy a car?
- Whether to take an expensive vacation?
- Whether to apply for a loan?
- How to allocate your 401K or other retirement investments?
- Whether to buy a particular stock that was touted to you?
- Which insurance company to choose?

For Each of the Decisions You List, Determine:

- The deadline for making the decision and the deadline for taking action on the decision.
- Whether the decision needs expert opinions, i.e., tax questions or finding the Moody's safety rating of a bond.
- Each of the actions you must take to get the expert advice you need to make the decision.

- Whether you and your significant other are, or may be, in conflict.
- The emotional reasons that interfere with the decision-making process, i.e., "I'm not lucky. Every time I buy a stock it goes down." Fear, greed, confusion. Ask yourself- is this feeling hurting my pocketbook? What is its origin? Can I afford to be self-indulgent about this feeling? How far away from my goals has this emotional barrier kept me?
- Write a sentence on what must be done to carry out the decision, once made. Is the implementation keeping you back? (i.e., you have no broker, it is too time-consuming.)

OK, now you have come face-to-face with where you are logically and where you are not in decision making. Let us see how well you do with logical advice on a very important decision when it comes to investing.

Let us look at when to sell a stock.

"This done, common sense, plus prudence, and minus piggishness, may determine the question and dictate the time for liquidation. This action, however, once decided upon must be adhered to with great rigidity, for thousands of traders who thus take time by the forelock have been dissatisfied afterwards by seeing a still greater advance in which they had no interests, and through greed and impatience have re- entered the lists in a most inopportune time."

The Pitfalls of Speculation, by Thomas Gibson, The Moody Corporation, 1906

I have focused on the decision of selling because it has many logical rules to help make that decision. I have set some of them out below. But, my real purpose in this is to have you read the logical selling signals below and think of a real asset of yours, a stock, even a house, and see how your emotions might tangle you up and prevent you from behaving logically.

But, let's remember first off that everyone has a philosophy to which they should be true. For example, Warren Buffet never sells a stock. His holding period is forever! But, most of us will do some buying and selling. So let's see the logic of it all.

When to Sell--The Logic of It

The greatest weakness of the individual investor is his or her failure to sell stocks when there is a profit to be had. Often, a good stock is selected, yet, no profit is ever taken. Or, if a stock is bad, the inexperienced investor hangs on too long, taking no action to limit his losses. This is clearly an emotional thing, like waiting for a miracle to save a bad marriage. How many times have you:

- Lost track and let the price slide down?
- Said to yourself, "When it comes back to this level I will sell it". Clearly, it never does.
- Watched for one more day without any reason than false hope?
- Let your profits run until the market changes and they disappear.

Important: The most successful investors follow this one simple rule - NEVER get emotionally attached to an investment (or a company's stock). Paper profits are not real, but paper losses are. You have to sell the stocks to get the profit.

Here are some of the logical things we look to in deciding whether it is time to sell:

- A drop in estimated earnings - get out!
- An actual drop in earnings (if you would not have bought the stock at this earning level) get out!
- An increase in insider selling.
- A technical signal says sell and you are near your profit target.

- A technical signal says sell, and you are not near your profit taking target. If that shows a sell signal too, do not wait.
- The stock is downgraded by analysts.
- And most importantly, why did you buy it in the first place and does it still suit your agenda?

Momentum vs. Value Investors

Warren Buffet is a value investor. He looks for companies whose total outstanding stock, if bought at current prices, would be less than the value of the company. He goes for bargains. When he buys a stock, he plans to keep it always. Right now, energy and commodities are in the value category. You can say they are underpriced.

Many investors like Buffet will buy these and hold. Others make some changes. But, the value investor looks through certain filters to select a stock; for example, price to earnings ratio and dividends in amount and consistency. They may change or add if they find companies with better value statistics.

The momentum buyer looks for stocks that are going up and measures that in many ways, including price rise pace, moving averages, stochastics and more. The momentum investor is not buying low and selling high, but buying high and selling even higher.

Have a strategy and stick with it. One investor in momentum stocks might place a 5% stop loss order (if the price dives by 2%, sell). Other great investors, like Jim O' Shaughnessy, author of *What Works on Wall Street*, have had 50% losses and have still outperformed the market by a huge margin.

Remember, no strategy will outperform the market every time, or in every incremental period.

As previously stated, always remember why you bought a stock. Most people forget. If the reason is no longer viable, get out.

When to Sell--Your Logic

The above was a battery of wisdom on the timing of stock selling. Did they strike you as too analytic, as too difficult to follow, as too cut and dry? What did you actually do when it came time to make a sell decision in the past? How did you behave? Did you act on logic? Where you regretful if the stock or other assets went up after the sale? DID YOU RIDE IT DOWN? Are you still deciding and took no action?

Is there room for improvement in your behavioral financial logic? Could we help you?

Ringing the Bell After Being Named a Barron's #1 Advisor

Chapter 9

Longevity and Behavioral Finance

Are you prepared to live to 125? No, really are you?

When I first wrote Logical Investing, 10,000 people a day reached the age of 60. Today 10,000 people a day reach age 65. We have a critical mass of retirees in our population. We have a new group of people who are chronologically older but not much biologically older. We have a new measure of age called HALE, Health Adjusted Life Expectancy. Actuaries no longer calculate insurance company ratings based solely on chronological age, but on biologic function.

A funny thing happened from the point of view of money because of our growing longevity.

People over 60 may live five years and reach 65, therefore, closer to taking retirement and closer to Social Security and pensions. But, they are not biologically five years older. They may be one year older physically and psychologically. So they feel just as good, they feel just as energetic as they did five years ago. They may want to do the same things, spend the same amount and fuel the same industries.

Yet, they have some critical financial decisions to make such as 401k distributions required by law, maximizing pensions, taking Social Security and how to fund insurance policies.

We are making decisions appropriate for the older adult when we have a younger mindset. We are realizing that our money must last much longer than expected. We knew this, but now the realization is hitting us because we are truly aware the fact of our aging. We always hoped we would live to 100 or more, but now baby boomers are beginning to realize that it is not a fantasy. It is possible, and we may not have the money for it.

This has an enormous impact on behavioral psychology. That impact is the fear that we might outlast our money.

Your financial advisor must realize that you are a younger person in a financially, chronologically older situation. You are making decisions before you are fundamentally ready to do so because you have to.

You are forced to do so by tax laws at age 70 ½ and by Social Security rules starting at age 62. It is likely that the fear of outliving your money will make you more fearful about your investments as well. That may lead you to very low or no risk investing.

There was a time that age 65 was the point at which you invested in fixed-income, at best, it was inflation indexed. You were not worried much about what would happen after 15 years because by then you probably would no longer be on this earth. Now, you are alive and your money needs growth as well.

Perhaps we should not reduce the level of risk in the portfolio just based on the age of the investor. Our thinking on this has changed just in the past few years. We allocate portfolios less conservatively due to our current low rate environment, but we must do so within the comfort zone of a client who fears risk because after retirement, they may not be able to make up for the loss.

Generally in times like these when investment grade corporate bonds and 10 and 30 year Treasuries are yielding around 2% and 3.5% and stock dividends are increasing to 4½%, there may be a great deal more stocks in a portfolio than bonds compared to prior decades. If you cannot take this type of risk, then you must realize flat out that you cannot live with the same spending lifestyle you have now.

A million dollars now can generate forty thousand dollars a year before taxes. Whereas before, when 10 year Treasuries were at 5% and corporate bonds were at 7%, which was fifty or seventy thousand dollars a year, there was a significant change in lifestyle for the very conservative investor.

Behavioral Psychology and Choosing Managers

I work hard to make sure that my clients understand what I look for not so much in a stock, bond or commodity, but in the manager that is selecting a security or asset for the asset class in which my client wants to invest. Examples of asset classes are value, growth, small and large caps. Within classes are the industries and offshore companies.

Because the choices from thousands of investment possibilities depend on the deep knowledge of the manager, I believe that selection and monitoring of managers are the most important things I do, and the most important message of this book. We are talking about the logic of investing, and yet we must rely on human beings to make our choices. How logical will our managers be?

I want managers to have skin in the game. If you do not invest in emerging markets yourself, how dare you suggest that anyone else does so? Investors feel good when the manager's financial future is also on the line with theirs.

An index or any ETF reflects the market. If my clients are going to pay money for active management, they are going to get active management. I am looking for managers that outperform the market over time.

I also look for managers that are consistent with their missions. If a good growth stock manager has been shifting or drifting toward value stocks, I want to know why. Does he or she really have the expertise to do so? In most cases, my default position is to get rid of the manager who has drifted from his expertise. If an excellent foreign investment manager starts to add domestic stocks with little background, I get concerned. More likely, a conservative manager may get more aggressive; again, I am watchful. The managers may even do a good job although drifting, but then the balance of the overall client's portfolio may get out of whack. That manager is still only one piece of a much larger pie. If you have five managers that drift away from their core styles, you'll never be able to get your hands around the overall risk of the portfolio, or benefit from your call to overweight a specific asset class. I make sure the asset allocation stays true.

For example, when I work with a client, we set parameters for risk and volatility. The risk is accessed by how much downside loss an investment might incur. We see if the risk tolerance is high, moderate or low. Then we look at the reward for the risk level and decide on parameters.

We also look at volatility which is the tendency for an asset to fluctuate in price and cause recurring changes in net worth. What is the tolerance there? Because these are so individual, a manager must stay in adherence to the parameters I set. Once the way the manager selects assets changes, I need to rethink my choice of managers. I can see whether, given the risk and volatility, a manager can outperform the indices. I reiterate that is my job. If you receive only market results, why bother with management and pay the fee?

I am not always looking for a manager with the most money in his or her strategy or protocol. In fact, this is often a negative, as the capital base of a fund grows, an asset manager needs to deploy more and more investor cash. A fund or portfolio could end up with 130 as contrasted with just 30 positions. The return from the 30 best will be diluted by the performance of the good, but not stellar 100. If the manager had fewer funds to invest, the trailing 100 would never make it into the account.

Smaller amounts under management allow for Tier 1 investments only, so you get the best of the best.

Few managers will close a fund and turn away investors (although some do.) The fact is, they earn a percentage of money under management. Every dollar has a pocketbook advantage to them; certainly 1% fee on five billion is better than 1% fee on one billion. You need not be a brilliant fund manager to do that math.

Certainly, I have additional criteria which include meeting and greeting, understanding the psychology of the manager and often their own personal background and even health condition. Managers are human beings, and they too are affected by humanistic issues.

For example, a recent Wall Street Journal article wrote of how a divorce can affect a manager's performance. http://www.wsj.com/articles/maybe-hedge-fund-data-should-include-the-managers-love-life-1428375828

When managers of hedge funds get divorced or married, it's bad news for their investors. Their asset returns are likely to suffer. Worse still, the pain could last years. That is the conclusion from a working research paper by academics at the University of Florida and Singapore Management University.

While the general news—that either event is distracting enough to lower job performance—might seem obvious, the paper goes further by answering the important questions: How much do investment returns suffer, and over what period? In short, returns get hit a lot, and the dip is long.

"We find that money managers significantly underperform during a divorce," states the paper."

Managers also run with the herd, play it safe and sometimes buy high and sell low. It is my job to watch them.

It is also my job to never be complacent. There are new brilliant managers on the horizon. I look for them and add them to my roster so that you can own a portfolio of brilliantly performing investments.

Chapter 10

Financial Assumptions and How We Create an Infrastructure for Decision Making

Frankly, I cannot imagine a more stressful scenario for a financial advisor (me) than planning for his parents. But, that is exactly what I did in an 83-page report.

I want to reveal to you how many areas of technical analysis, asset allocation, and even tax planning go into creating an infrastructure to make ongoing investment decisions with Bite. These decisions include the allocation into asset classes, then the sub-accounts in each class, then the individual investments in each sub-account. I used my own parents' plan and the instructive language from it to help you make the connection between your temperament - which is emotional - and to apply it to inform and impact the logical decisions you make.

Warning: This Chapter is technical. It encompasses many facts, processes and definitions regarding investing. I use very elaborate processes to stress test all of my clients, and certainly my parents' plan, before I advise and manage. We have put the material from our reports in more simple language and hope you will read it as it is for your education. But, I understand if it seems heavy going. If so, look at the REASON we have offered you this material - to show you how your temperament affects your decision-making logic.

Rate of Return Methodology

If you plan to make financial decisions, you will want to compare the rate of return you will get from one investment choice to another. There are several methods for determining the expected rates of return that any given investment will yield. The method you select to calculate the rate of return is a function of your level of conservative vs. risk-taking behavior.

Here is a simple way to understand this. Let's say you own a portfolio of bonds with an expected return of 5% and a portfolio of stocks with a long-term assumption of expected returns of 9%. Your portfolio is 50% in the bond, 50% in the stock. Your expected rate of return is 7%; the average of 5 and 9.

You can change your expected rate of return by increasing stocks and decreasing bonds, or reduce your rate of return by increasing bonds and decreasing stock.

Why would you want to do the later? Simply because the higher rate of return will likely also take on more risk of loss.

Put another way, the reaction you have to loss and profit dictates how you will choose a method of projecting returns and whether you will have CONFIDENCE in that method or not. If you have confidence in your method of decision making, you are likely to withstand the tempests caused by market news reports. If you lack confidence in the way that any aspect of your plan is calculated, you are likely to be panicked or "manicked" by market news and grow uncomfortable with your plan.

Here's an investment point that I find significant - the concept of 'standard deviation' (measuring how far an investment might deviate in price from the norm). Funds prices deviate from time to time. If they deviate a great deal from the average of their class of funds, they are a more volatile asset in your portfolio and are best for more active traders who can watch and take profits.

I like the math of standard deviation. But, if you are not a financial math nerd like me, perhaps you can have some fun with this from www.mathsisfun.com:

Standard Deviation

The Standard Deviation is a measure of how spread out numbers are.

Its symbol is σ (the Greek letter sigma).

The formula is easy: it is the **square root** of the **Variance**. So now you ask, "What is the Variance?"

Variance

The Variance is defined as:

The average of the **squared** differences from the Mean.

To calculate the variance, follow these steps:

- Work out the Mean (the simple average of the numbers)
- Then for each number: subtract the Mean and square the result (the *squared difference*).
- Then work out the average of those squared differences. (Why Square?)

Example

You and your friends have just measured the heights of your dogs (in millimeters):

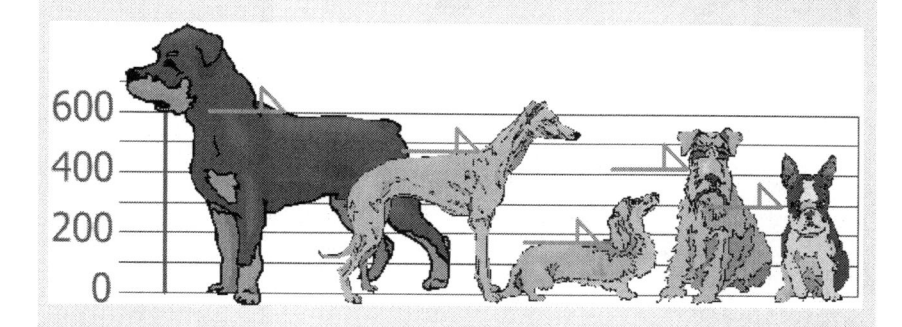

The heights (at the shoulders) are: 600mm, 470mm, 170mm, 430mm and 300mm.

Find out the Mean, the Variance, and the Standard Deviation.

Your first step is to find the Mean: Answer:

Mean = (600 + 470 + 170 + 430 + 300)/5 = 1970/5 = 394

so the mean (average) height is 394 mm.

Let's plot this on the chart:

Now we calculate each dog's difference from the Mean:

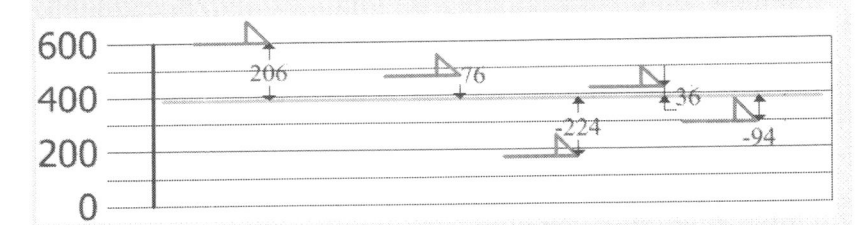

To calculate the Variance, take each difference, square it, and then average the result:

$$\text{Variance: } \sigma^2 = \frac{206^2 + 76^2 + (-224)^2 + 36^2 + (-94)^2}{5}$$

$$= \frac{42{,}436 + 5{,}776 + 50{,}176 + 1{,}296 + 8{,}836}{5}$$

$$= \frac{108{,}520}{5} = 21{,}704$$

So, the Variance is **21,704**.

And the Standard Deviation is just the square root of Variance, so:

Standard Deviation: σ = √**21,704** = **147.32...** = **147** (to the nearest mm)

And the good thing about the Standard Deviation is that it is useful. Now we can show which heights are within one Standard Deviation (147mm) of the Mean:

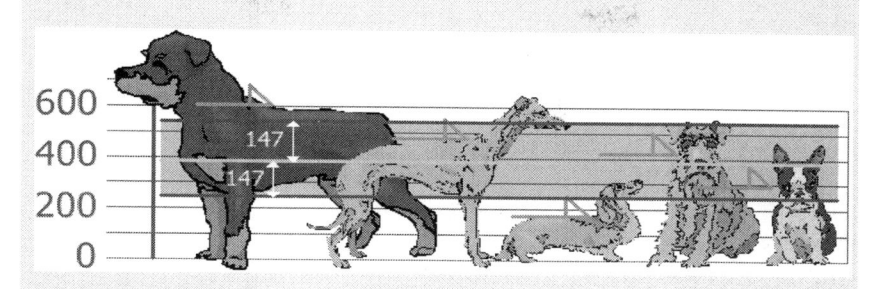

So, using the Standard Deviation we have a "standard" way of knowing what is normal, and what is extra large or extra small.

Rottweilers **are** tall dogs. And Dachshunds **are** a bit short ... but don't tell them!

I have found that when a client understands standard deviations, they get less stressed with price changes, understand better their level of risk, and understand better why I am making portfolio adjustments.

There are at least TWO methods of projecting Rate of Return. Which one seems most appropriate for you?

1. Historical returns, a strict look at the past. Projected returns based on the historical return averages. We use broad market indices like the S&P 500, the Dow, and a bond index that represents different asset classes.

2. Proprietary formulas which take historical return averages of the broad market indices, as above, and adjusts them in light of current market conditions and other factors. There is the thought of human forecasters behind any of these formulas.

Do you prefer the human intelligence factor or do you want your calculations to be based solely on verifiable past numbers? In which do you have greater confidence? It is up to you.

There are other choices as well. But, you can see how the way you THINK will dictate even the most analytic and technical part of financial planning.

What If Scenarios

For my parents, I used three methods of calculating rate of return, each of which provides one outcome from a wide range of possible outcomes. Here are the three ways we calculated returns, as expressed by Morgan Stanley Smith Barney, which I used on my parents' plan:

The methods used were:

- "Average Returns," calculated using one average return for their pre-retirement period and one average return for their post-retirement period.

- "Historical Test," calculated by using the actual historical returns and inflation rates, in sequence, from a starting year to the present, and assumes that they would receive those returns and inflation rates, in sequence, from this year through the end of their analysis.

- "Historical Rolling Periods," a series of Historical Tests, each of which uses the actual historical returns and inflations rates, in sequence, from a starting year to an ending year, and assumes that they would receive those returns and inflation rates, in sequence, from this year through the end of their analysis. Rolling Period Results are calculated using only three asset classes -- Cash, Bonds, and Stocks. Specifically:

    Cash - Ibbotson US 30 Treasury Bills (1926-2010)

    Bonds - Ibbotson Intermediate-Term Government Bonds - Total Return (1926-2010)

Stocks - Ibbotson Large Company Stocks - Total Return (1926-2010).

This is nearly identical to how I would calculate today.

So, how does your temperament or behavioral finance profile dictate which of these technical calculations to apply in calculating your projected rate of return?

Let us see.

Results with Bad Timing

If you are very risk averse, you want to calculate what will happen if the market falls upon hard times. What is important is not so much that you can do this type of calculation, or even understand it, but that you are CONFIDENT that these bad times are under consideration. So when they strike, if they do, you never panic. It is very much like our session with Wayne Chrebet when he told us how the football players rely on trends, but EXPECT and plan for the unexpected during a play.

If that type of event happens, ask what is your next step and are you comfortable taking it? If not, you may need to redo your plan to avoid that type of volatility. If you have 50% in stocks and the market fell and you lost 20% of your stock portfolio, are you comfortable adding to that portfolio? If 'yes,' you may be a good candidate for a long run positive result. If not, you are a better candidate for less risk, as you may simply bail out in a slump and never recover. That is why we test to see the reaction you have in bad times.

Results with bad timing are calculated by projecting low returns for at least a few years in the future. If you want to be very conservative, make those years the first ones in which you make your withdrawals. This is also why it is not a good idea to withdraw more in the early years of your retirement; there is less of a chance to grow if there is less in the beginning.

If your head is spinning, let us get to the bottom line: if you want to plan your future based on the most conservative rate of return projection, take into consideration bad times. Then you need to adjust your expectations accordingly. There are many other ways of calculating returns. We have discussed many of them already, and I have included some of the most used below. But, they all add up to this: work with your advisor to be sure that they calculate returns in a way in which you will have continued confidence in your plan. That is all you need.

A short glossary of ways of calculating rate of return:

Results Using Class Sensitivity

If you are heavily invested in one asset class, calculate how that would affect your portfolio if the entire class had several bad years. It might spark a more diverse allocation.

Results Using Monte Carlo Simulations

The computer has helped us enormously in making calculations that use past performance and change variables to give you a better idea of the actual results you can expect under different conditions. Like knowing what to do in the football field when it starts to pour.

A Monte Carlo simulation takes into account changes in the rate of return on your investments and does multiple calculations to see the effect on risk and return to show how variations each year can affect your results. A Monte Carlo simulation calculates the results of your allocation by running it many times, using a different sequence of returns each time. You see under which circumstances you would have met all your goals and in which you would not have met your goals. The percentage of trials that were successful shows the probability that your allocation will be successful.

Analogously, the percentage of trials that were unsuccessful is shown as the Probability of Failure. By the way, my program allowed me to Monte Carlo Test 10,000 variations.

Only You Can Determine Your Comfort Level

After we calculate the expected return and see how that might fair in a bad-timing analysis, we have a figure that tells you how close or far an investment strategy will get you to your goal. We answer the critical question: Do you have enough money to live the life you love? If you do, congratulations. If you do not, you will need to reassess some of your life variables like:

- How much you intend to spend
- How long you intend to work
- How much risk you are willing to take
- Where you will live
- How much debt you are willing to carry

That is the impact on your life of making hard decisions based on as close to accurate future projections as possible.

Are You Super Conservative Like My Parents?

In my parents' case, the projections showed that they would be able to meet the expenses that they expected without running out of money. Still, my parents weren't satisfied. Well, at least, my mother wasn't satisfied. And you know what that means. I needed to assure both my Mom and Dad. So I looked at "safety margin."

The safety margin is the estimated value of your assets at the end of the analysis period, based on all the assumptions you have made. Only you can determine if that safety margin is sufficient for your needs. In my parents' case, they wanted more assurances. A great deal of that has to do with your EXPECTATION of lifespan and your expenses.

Today we also look at your HALE - Health Adjusted Life Expectancy to see how far out we must project, if you are in danger of running out of money if you live past

100, and, also, how much likelihood there is of your needing expensive long-term care in the future.

Then we apply a bear market test using cash, bonds and stocks to see the effect of a prolonged recession on your portfolio.

So, with all that work, could I GUARANTEE that my own parents will get the exact result we calculated? NO, NO, NO.

Why not?

Here are four good reasons why not:

#1. 100% accurate prediction is a myth: It is important to remember that future rates of return cannot be predicted with certainty and that investments that may provide higher rates of return are generally subject to higher risk and volatility. The actual rate of return on investments can vary widely over time. This includes the potential loss of principal on your investment.

#2. We use indices for calculations, but you cannot invest in a pure index: Indices illustrate the investment performance of instruments that have certain similar characteristics and are intended to reflect broad segments of an asset class. Indices do not represent the actual or hypothetical performance of any specific investment, including any individual security within an index.

Although some indices can be replicated, it is not possible to directly invest in an index. It is important to remember the investment performance of an index does not reflect deductions for investment charges, expenses or fees that may apply when investing in securities and financial instruments such as commissions, sales loads or other applicable fees. Also, the stated investment performance assumes the reinvestment of interest and dividends at net asset value without taxes, and also assumes that the portfolio is consistently "rebalanced" to the initial target weightings.

"Rebalancing" describes the discipline of selling assets and buying others to match the target weightings of an asset allocation model. Because assets increase and decrease in value over time, the percentage amounts of assets invested in each class will tend to vary from their original target weightings.

#3. Asset allocations are a moving target over time: Asset allocations that deviate significantly from the initial weightings can significantly affect the likelihood of achieving the projected investment performance.

#4. *Individual stocks can surprise you:* Another important factor to keep in mind when considering the historical and projected returns of indices is that the risk of loss in value of a specific asset, such as a stock, a bond or a share of a mutual fund, is not the same as, and does not match, the risk of loss in a broad asset class index.

As a result, the investment performance of an index will not be the same as the investment performance of a specific instrument, including one that is contained in the index. Such a possible lack of "investment performance correlation" may also apply to the future of a specific instrument relative to an index.

Financial Forecasting--Bark or Bite?

Where have you heard this before?

"As always, keep in mind that past performance is no guarantee of future results. These are for illustrative purposes only and are not indicative of the future performance of any specific investment."

Take a look at how we see the limitations and the benefits of financial forecasting. Put simply, we are saying that we do our best, and we think our best is better than others.

Allocate and Diversify: Here is one way to get closer to making the reality of a portfolio closer to the predicted results.

Performance of an asset class within a portfolio is dependent upon the allocation of securities within the asset class and the weighting or the percentage of the asset class within that portfolio. Potential for a portfolio's loss is exacerbated in a downward trending market. A well-diversified portfolio is less vulnerable in a falling market.

We use this list of published indices to determine an allocation projection:

- Cash - USD (90-day Tbills) Bloomberg US Generic Government 3 Month Yield
- Global Govt/Govt-Related Bonds (hedged to USD) Barclays Capital Global Aggregate: Govt/Govt-Related (hedged to USD)
- Global Corporate/Securitized Bonds (hedged to USD)
- Barclays Capital Global Aggregate: Corporate/Securitized (hedged to USD)
- Global Short-Term Government Bonds (hedged to USD)
- Barclays Capital Global Treasury (1-3 Year) (hedged to USD)
- Global High Yield Bonds (hedged to USD) Barclays Capital Global High Yield (hedged to USD)
- Global Emerging Markets Local Debt (unhedged) JPM GBI-EM Global Diversified Composite (unhedged USD)
- US Large-Cap Value Stocks Russell 1000 Value
- US Large-Cap Growth Stocks Russell 1000 Growth
- US Mid-Cap Value Stocks Russell Mid-Cap Value
- US Mid-Cap Growth Stocks Russell Mid-Cap Growth
- US Small-Cap Value Stocks Russell 2000 Value
- US Small-Cap Growth Stocks Russell 2000 Growth
- Developed-Market ex US Small-Cap Stocks MSCI World ex US Small-Cap (unhedged)

- Europe ex UK Large/Mid-Cap Stocks (unhedged) MSCI Europe ex UK Standard
- UK Large/Mid-Cap Stocks (unhedged) MSCI UK Standard
- Japan Large/Mid-Cap Stocks (unhedged) MSCI Japan Standard
- Canada Large/Mid-Cap Stocks (unhedged) MSCI Canada Standard
- Dev Asia Pacific ex Japan Lrg/Mid-Stocks MSCI Pacific ex Japan Standard (unhedged)
- Global Emerging Market Stocks (unhedged) MSCI EMF IMI
- Global REITs (unhedged) FTSE EPRA NAREIT Global Total Return
- Commodities DJ/UBS Commodity Total Return
- Global Inflation-Linked Securities (hedged to USD) Barclays Capital Global Inflation-Linked (hedged to USD)
- Broad Fund of Hedge Funds MS AIP, HFRI Fund of Funds Composite
- Managed Futures Barclay BTop50
- US Private Equity MSSB Global Investment Strategy, Venture Economics
- US Private Real Estate Funds

So, is the possibility of making accurate future projections a Bark or a Bite?

If you are looking for guarantees, that cannot be provided by anyone. If you are looking for assumptions and projections upon which logical conclusions can be based, we can create that system and implement it for you.

Alternative Investments

We also work with alternative investments for those less risk averse, and/or with larger portfolios, for those who are particularly interested in a niche sector or alternative ways of investing, and who do not need liquidity. Here are a few types of so-called alternative investments with indications of the type of risk you might be taking when you invest:

Hedge Funds break down into various hedged strategies with different characteristics. They may be highly illiquid, can engage in leverage, short-selling and other speculative practices that may increase volatility and the risk of loss, and may be subject to large investment minimums and initial lock-ups. They may involve complex tax structures, tax inefficient investing and delays in distributing important tax information.

Managed futures are commodity pools managed by professional Commodity Trading Advisors ("CTAs"), who typically trade futures, interbank currency forwards, options on futures and forwards.

Private Equity Funds typically invest in securities, instruments, and assets that are not, and are not expected to become publicly traded, and therefore may require a substantial length of time to realize a return or fully liquidate. They typically have high management, performance and placement fees which can lower the returns achieved by investors.

Commodity markets may fluctuate widely based on a variety of factors including changes in supply and demand relationships, governmental programs and policies, national and international political and economic events, war and terrorist events, changes in interest and exchange rates, trading activities in commodities and related contracts; pestilence, weather, technological change, and the price volatility of a commodity.

Derivatives, in general, involve special risks and costs that may result in losses. The successful use of derivatives requires sophisticated management in order to manage and analyze derivatives transactions. The prices of derivatives may move in unexpected ways, especially in abnormal market conditions. Some derivatives are "leveraged" and therefore may magnify or otherwise increase investment losses. Other risks include the potential inability to terminate or sell derivative positions, as a result of counterparty failure to settle or other reasons.

Investing in **fixed-income securities** involves interest rate risk, credit risk and inflation risk. Interest rate risk is the possibility that bond prices will decrease because of an interest rate increase. When interest rates rise, bond prices, and the values of fixed-income securities generally fall. Credit risk is the risk that a company will not be able to pay its debts, including the interest on its bonds. Inflation risk is the possibility that the interest paid on an investment in bonds will be lower than the inflation rate, decreasing purchasing power.

High Yield Fixed-Income Securities, also known as "junk bonds", are considered speculative, involve greater risk of default and tend to be more volatile than investment grade fixed-income securities.

International/Emerging Markets Equities--Foreign investing involves certain risks not typically associated with investments in domestic corporations and obligations issued by the US Government, such as currency fluctuations and controls, restrictions on foreign investments, less governmental supervision and regulation, less liquidity and the potential for market volatility and political instability. In addition, the securities markets of many of the emerging markets are substantially smaller, less developed, less liquid and more volatile than the securities of the US and other more developed countries.

Long/Short --Using a short sales strategy in combination with long positions in an attempt to improve performance may result in greater losses or lower positive returns than if the positions held were long only, thus creating the potential for unlimited losses.

Mortgage-Backed Securities are subject to faster or slower prepayments than expected on underlying mortgage loans, which can dramatically alter the yield-to-maturity of a mortgage-backed security. They are also subject to prepayment risk. When interest rates fall, an issuer may choose to borrow money at a lower interest rate, while paying off its previously issued bonds.

As a consequence, underlying bonds will lose the interest payments from the investment and will be forced to reinvest in a market where prevailing interest rates are lower than when the initial investment was made. Asset-backed securities generally decrease in value as a result of interest rate increases, but may benefit less than other fixed-income securities from declining interest rates, principally because of prepayments.

Non-US Fixed-Income--Foreign fixed-income securities may involve greater risks than those issued by US companies or the US Government. Economic, political and other events unique to a country or region will affect those markets and their issues, but may not affect the US market or similar US issuers.

The Private equity real estate asset class may involve special investment considerations, including investor net asset minimum criteria, investment vehicle entry and exit conditions, regulatory, tax reporting and/or compliance requirements, and suitability guidelines.

REITs--In addition to the general risks associated with real estate investments, REIT investing entails other risks such as credit and interest rate risk. Real estate investment risks can include fluctuations in the value of underlying properties, defaults by borrowers or tenants, market saturation, changes in general and local economic conditions, decreases in market rates for rents, increases in competition, property taxes, capital expenditures, or operating expenses, and other economic, political or regulatory occurrences affecting the real estate industry.

Small/Mid-Cap Equity--Stocks of small and medium-sized companies entail special risks, such as limited product lines, markets, financial resources, greater market volatility than securities of larger, and more established companies.

Small/Mid-Cap Equity--Stocks of small and medium-sized companies entail special risks, such as limited product lines, markets, and financial resources, and greater market volatility than securities of larger, more established companies.

Stocks--Investing in stock securities involves volatility risk, market risk, business risk, and industry risk because the prices of stocks fluctuate.

Volatility risk is the chance that the value of a stock will fall.

Market risk is the chance that the prices of all stocks will fall due to conditions in the economic environment.

Business risk is the chance that a specific company's stock will fall because of issues affecting it such as the way the company is managed.

Industry risk is the chance that a set of factors particular to an industry group will adversely affect stock prices within the industry."

Thank you to the folks at Morgan Stanley Smith Barney for so understandably defining these hard to grasp asset classes.

Now, how do you decide if an alternative investment should be in your portfolio?

You are catching on - you look at your risk tolerance, as we will do in the next Chapter.

Chapter 11

How Are You With Risk?

"They can give reasons for their ventures, but they are without foundation, and are no more worthy of consideration than the reasons by the roulette 'player' for 'staking' upon a certain number."

The Pitfalls of Speculation, by Thomas Gibson, The Moody Corporation, 1906

That is why I devote an entire Chapter to only one area of money management – risk tolerance. If I make money for my client, I might get a referral and a smile. If I lose money for my client, I most likely have lost the client.

How do I know how to help clients make a decision with regard to risk?

Let us say I have two clients, and we have worked out their personal expenses and their incomes. They have discovered that in order for their expenses to be met using interest from their investments, they both need an 8% annualized return. Let us say that one client cannot tolerate the risk of loss. The other is less risk averse, maybe because he has more years to make up for losses, or maybe he has untapped sources of income, making losses less stressful.

Would I suggest that they both choose an 8% return and the volatility that comes with it if that had a risk component?

The answer is "no" because even though their financial needs are the same, their risk tolerance is very different. In a stress scenario, I cannot count on the risk adverse client to stay with the program and not bail out at the first sign of decline, wiping cut years of returns.

Even though most of our accounts are discretionary, and I may not want to make a disastrous sale, the client has the right to sell out the account and take their business elsewhere.

The stock market is really an auction. One day out of hundreds, there will be people who simply do not come to the auction. 98% of the time, the market will be efficient. But, if you panic and cannot withstand the one day when it is inefficient, you must be careful about your risk tolerance

Here is a literally "homey" analogy that might resonate with you.

Let us go back to the analogy of the people who live near a beautiful beach. They love the scenery. They have withstood flooding from the ocean. But, now they have grown older. They can no longer withstand the stress of temporarily moving out of the home, having cleanup men come to their house, having their memories soaked in water, buying new furniture and moving back.

Perhaps it is wise to sell and get out.

Of course, this is a metaphor for being more conservative after retirement.

Similarly, let us say you are a young couple with small babies and school-aged children whose lives would be disrupted by a flood. The flood would damage their childhood memories. If you are the type who's scared of floods, make sure you do not live in a floodplain no matter how beautiful and inexpensive the home.

Neither couple might want to live in such a house. High-risk investments are like a house in a floodplain. It is likely that you got a bargain and a great value. But, related stresses may not make the return worth it to you.

This homey example of financial behavior happens all the time. I use managers with specific expertise so they can pick up "bargains" and have an infrastructure to pounce on a bargain, because they know their sector on a granular level in a narrow area of expertise. I want to work with people who are the masters of their areas, not a jack of all trades.

Sure, they often outperform the market, but it is only logical that I choose to take risks only where it is appropriate for a particular client. I call it "the market of YOU."

Now, it is time to really search your financial soul and own up to the type of risk taker you are:

- Scared rabbit
- Cautious, but game
- Cowboy

Be honest with yourself. Determine who you are and share it with your advisor, your co-decision maker, and look at each investment through the lens of your risk behavioral profile.

I KNOW WHAT YOU MAY BE THINKING. Can I have great returns and lower risk, too?

Well, sometimes know-how and logic reduces risk and keeps returns high.

One example is the Closed End Fund.

Tactical Uses of Closed End Funds to Boost Returns and Control Risk

Closed End Funds (CEF) can be a very useful tool in certain instances and add dramatically to the performance of a specific asset class allocation. Their imbedded inefficiencies can be exploited for large gains and in many cases without huge risks. I use Closed End Funds in my various discretionary models as tactical trades to juice returns.

Let us first look at the structure itself. A Closed End Fund is basically a basket of marketable securities that individually trade on various exchanges based on supply and demand. When you buy a Closed End Fund, you are buying someone's shares. You can invest in this basket or portfolio, and thus, the basket itself (CEF) trades on supply and demand as well.

This creates two prices. One is called the NAV (Net Asset Value), which is the total market value of all of the securities in the CEF. If you divide that number by the number of shares the CEF has in the basket, you will get the NAV per share. The market price per share of the CEF and NAV price per share can differ dramatically at times and thus an opportunity arises.

Closed End Funds can vary in style and complexity; but for the sake of simplicity, let us look at just a few real examples.

Municipal Bond CEF

Some of the simplest forms of CEF are the ones that invest in municipal bonds. As an example I would like to use "NIO," Nuveen Insured Municipal Opportunity. As its name implies, it invests in insured municipal bonds.

In the fall of 2008, this fund traded at 33% discount to its NAV. A fixed-income portfolio manager could buy a $100k individual municipal bond or a $100k municipal CEF like NIO for $70k, since it was trading at a 30% discount.

NIO was yielding 7.8% tax-free. One month later NAV discount was 10%; and, therefore, even if the NAV stayed the same, the investors would have made 20% return in munis!! In fact, if you held this CEF for just 6 months, your return would have been 47% or 125% annualized inclusive of dividends. This was even more pronounced in "VTJ," Investco Van Kampen, and "NPP," a thinner volume CEF. All three eventually traded at premiums to NAV.

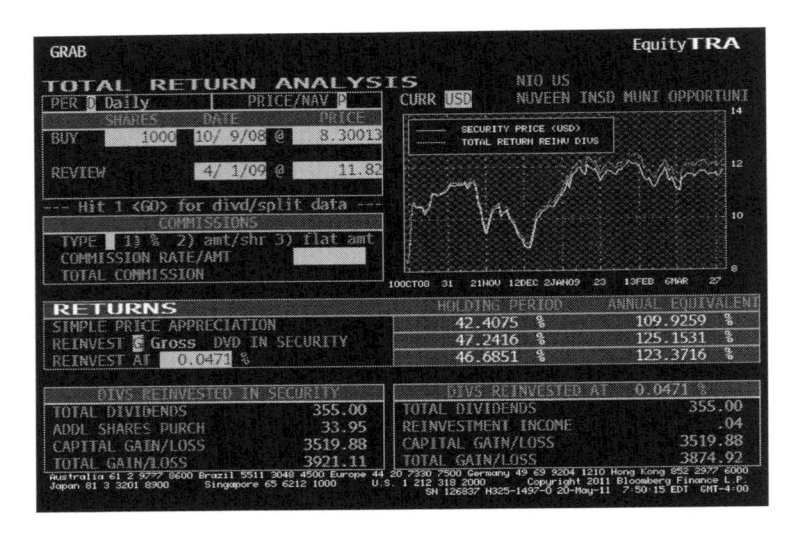

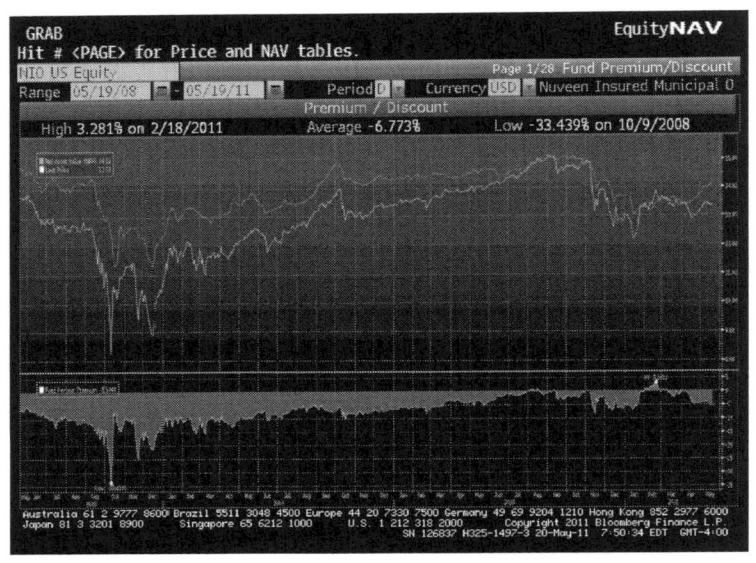

The chart shows a return of 42% in one quarter, annualized yield 125%. The fund sold for over 30% below NAV. This demonstrates the difference between the value of an investment as contrasted with its price. Sometimes, that is the way to get both lower risk and higher returns.

The Tactic

The conclusion is that if you are going to go along the municipal market (expect that bond prices will rise) and do not mind some extra volatility, why not complement your strategy with discounted CEFs?

CEFs, for the most part, are products that are traded by the retail public. Rarely do you find institutional investors holding large positions of CEF.

Most CEFs lack the necessary volume needed for easy accumulation and sale by institutions. This magnifies the price inefficiencies and makes inefficiencies endure longer than they would have otherwise. A thinly traded municipal CEF could easily be knocked down 10% with relatively small sales volume.

So we watch for thinly traded CEFs that may increase volatility.

Trading Platform and Execution Advantage

As a portfolio manager running discretionary accounts, there are advantages that I enjoy in the area of CEFs. I can react quickly on behalf of all of my clients simultaneously. If, however, I was running my business as a classic broker, I would need to get on the phone and call each client individually first. This process can take days and the pricing could be lost. Who gets the first call, and who gets the last call? A firm with a great research department and a large number of financial advisors can make these products move solely based upon their recommendations. I want all my clients to be in front of the line if a gem is uncovered or a rotten apple is exposed.

Be Careful of Yield Traps

Due to short-term rates being near zero today, many investors have been buying up CEFs based on the yield. Let us remember that many of these funds often use leverage up to 30%. Therefore, a fund yielding 5% that is levered 30%, without leverage would yield 3.8%. (3.8% times 1.3). Currently there are CEFs in the fixed-income and MLP arena that have moved up due to investors' appetite for yield.

Some of the largest ones are trading at 15% premium to NAV while yielding in the 6.5% area, and they are levered. As interest rates rise and investors see that they can get much better rates while being higher up on the capital structure, a levered yield of 6.5% will no longer suffice.

An exodus could easily cause a 15% premium to go to 10% discount. That will be a 25% loss even before factoring in the lower price of the actual securities within the fund.

An important moral: Know the difference between true value and borrowed value. That is the wisdom of the mature investor.

Part of that maturity is getting clarity on the facts of your own wealth. We will turn our attention to that in the next Chapter.

Memorable Moments

Live On the Air--Fox Business News

Ed's First Book, "Logical Investing" First Edition

Ed Ranks in Barron's Top 100 Advisors

Memorable Moments

Golfing Day--Donald Trump with Ed, the golf pro, and Wayne Chrebet

Ring of Honor Inductee--Wayne Chrebet with Partners Ed and Jimmy Lee

First Book Signing: Joe Tahmoosh, Mary Bennett, Jimmy Lee, Eve & Ed Moldaver, Adriane Berg, Mary Sliwa, Wayne Chrebet and, Mark O'Shea

Lunch with Larry Kudlow, discussing the economy with Governor Paterson, Mary Sliwa, Ed Moldaver and Jimmy Lee

Michael Strahan, a very special guest at our office.

Heisman 2015

Chapter 12

Know What You Are Worth

I am happy to say that the majority of my clients have a very good idea of their personal wealth, their needs and their goals. Most people who have achieved wealth have a good handle on today's expenditures, income and all-important cash flow.

Successful people have a genuine and healthy interest in their own money. They are not bored by making budgets or reading some of the books that I suggest. Sometimes, though, I find that clients with $5 million or less generally know what they spend, but people with more than $5 million, particularly if their wealth comes from high earnings like our sports figure clients, often lose track of their wealth.

I know that the press and their fans often fault big name athletes for this money madness. But, I do not. People at this level of wealth most often cannot handle the business of their own wealth, and so they hire an advisor. These advisors lose track and control of their client's money; they overuse leverage, take loans on their investment portfolio, all of which exposes their clients to undue risk, and in some cases losses of more billions than I can count.

Whatever your level of wealth, we will not allow that to happen to you. In Appendix I of this book, you will find a simple chart to give a handle on your financial picture. I hope you bring this with you when we have our first consultation. But, even if you never meet with us, or any advisor, I urge you to have certain documents on hand and really review them.

Here are the documents we look for and ask you to bring to your initial meetings:

- Your last two years of income tax returns
- Recent financial statements prepared for any refinancing of your home or business

- Current bank statements
- Current mutual fund statements
- Current brokerage statements
- Current mortgage statements
- Current life insurance policies
- Current employee benefit statements, including 401(k) and other retirement plans
- Wills/trusts
- Powers of attorney
- Health care proxies or living wills
- Anything else that you think is important that you work with on a regular basis when it comes to finance.

Five Steps to Take Now to Get Clarity on Your Own Wealth

- **STEP #1**-Get your financial house in order. Gather together the documents you would "rescue" in case of a fire, i.e., insurance policies, the power of attorney your mother signed, your will, car related documents, leases, etc. It is useful to close your eyes and imagine what you would need. Then, gather them together in one handy place. This is also the time to consider a safe-deposit box for little used important documents. What do you not have? An updated passport, a will?

- **STEP #2**-Make a cash flow calendar. Take a current calendar. Note the dates at which big sums come due - insurance premiums, rent, monthly mortgage, tuition, vacation, etc. Note the months that big sums come in, tax refunds, yearly trust distributions, royalties, rents, a company bonus. Just eyeball it and share it with your co-decision maker. That gets you a real lead on what your financial year looks like for cash flow planning.

- **STEP #3**-Make a list of all your assets and liabilities.

- **STEP #4**-Make a quick expense statement (euphemism for budget). People earning over $100,000 a year and spending over 70% of their income can usually cut down expenses without reducing quality of life.

- **STEP #5**-Review your insurance policies, all of them! Most people are underinsured. Have enough death benefits to pay off your mortgage, college, major debts and leave the family enough death benefit to produce at least 60% of your current gross income. To build a legacy, use second to die insurance. When you are in your mid-to-late 50's, or if you are already older, make an appointment to review long-term health care policies. If you are over 60, buy disability insurance. Add an umbrella policy.

Congratulations. Now you are clearheaded. You have clarity around your risk tolerance, your wealth picture and a plan.

Ringing the NASDAQ Closing Bell with Lifeway Foods.

Part III: Fluff, Bark, Bite, Bite, Bite

Chapter 13

Beware of the Gray Brochure - The Fluff

A company brochure is very easy to write. And a fund manager is an easy title to have. But there is a difference between a manager of funds and the manager that is managing the managers.

I am a selector of fund managers for my clients. I chose the managers and present the reasons why I have chosen them. It is my job to come up with specific asset classes from which the client would most benefit. We know what they are. Every wealth manager has access to every one of them. The skill is in crafting the portfolio to work for you.

Within each asset class, I can choose from a number of funds managed differently. Or, I can simply choose an index and reduce management fees. Yes, I do make a connection between fees and results. I have one job and that is to beat the indices. If I cannot do that, why would you bother working with me? Part of that result is the net cost of management. I look at all the results and, also, at the net result after the cost to you.

How do I judge the results to be expected when selecting a fund manager?

By law, we must tell you that past results do not dictate future performance. In fact, that is not just the law. It is also true. Some of the best performing managers over the previous five years end up having the worst performance over the following five years.

Each moment in time takes independent thought as to what managers are doing and whether they are doing it well enough to beat the index and are worth their cost.

Through the years, I have discovered a secret. There are certain characteristics that managers have in common which do enable them to beat an index, and to continue to do so. There are clues to discovering which ones may perform best and also which ways of thinking might hold them back.

Here is a reprise of some of the criteria I use to judge a manager:

Are they part of the fund company they are running? We want them to have ownership and skin in the game. We want their fortunes to rise and fall with yours.

How does the manager create results? Who are their reference groups and their mentors? What type of research and from whom does that research come on which they rely? If they manage emerging growth country funds, have they traveled? Or, who travels on their behalf? Who are their ears and eyes? As you know from my past comments on the distractions of divorce and family issues as effects on the clear thinking of the fund manager, their personal life is a huge factor as well.

If they have been doing very well, has the team changed? If so, this is a red flag.

Has the CEO left? Management change always gives me pause.

How many types of companies do they include in the funds' portfolios? It takes much more skill and personnel to correctly select 130 stocks than to study and select 30. Further, of course, the more stocks you have in a portfolio of the same asset class the more 'index hugging' your results will be.

There is not necessarily safety in numbers. There is usually just mediocrity in numbers when it comes to the number of investments in a managed portfolio.

Here is an example of what happened just the other day. A prospective client told me he was in a fund that just closed. He got a notice of closure; but because he was already in the fund, he would still be allowed to make contributions. He asked me whether it was as good a fund after it closed to new investors as it was before.

I explained that the fund had too much money and no place that the fund manager thought was worthy to park that money. They did not want to take any more investors and dilute the performance of the fund by buying 'B' list securities. Or it might end up looking like an index instead of beating an index.

Now, for an index fund, you will pay about 1/10 of 1% as a fee. But, for an actively managed fund, you might pay ½% to 2% in fees. What is the point if the managed account will not beat an index?

As for the gentleman's question, the closing of the fund could be good news or bad news.

It depends on why they closed. If they already were too large, then he will probably not see the results he did in the past. I would not put in more money. If there is a history of this manager doing well and closing funds at the right time, the closing is a bonus. That is what I mean by knowing the fund manager intimately.

This does not always mean we follow the good fund managers wherever they go.

For example, I have seen many a brilliant fund manager in one niche crossover to another niche and lose his or her shirt. Just because somebody is brilliant in one area and understands a specific asset class does not mean it is going to carry over to a different fund with a different style. I do tend to get out of funds when there is change or drift.

("The drift" refers, for example, to a manager with a large-cap mandate buying non-large-cap stocks and, therefore, drifting from the mandate.) I do not want to take the risk of a change.

The managers I select are not in their own bubble. He or she is part of a much larger picture. My customized allocation for each client can be thrown off by a manager unilaterally adding an international stock to a domestic strategy. This knocks my allocation out of whack. So I may change the manager.

On the other hand, when I've worked with the manager for a while and he or she has been consistent, I can tolerate losses. A good manager might underperform for a period of time against his benchmark. That is par for the course. But, I also know that over time, he or she may outperform the market 70% of the time. I give them a chance for a while because I have seen his or her behavior when it is time to rally. No one outperforms the market every year or in any given year.

An example is James O'Shaughnessy. In any given year he outperformed the market by 70%. His 'rolling year average' (how much he outperformed over a period of years), is 95% over any given three years and 99% over any given five years. Now you know why I keep referring to him. If he underperforms in one year, I don't panic. I wait for the rally. And I monitor the performance of every manager I select to see how if they outperform the market.

I am pretty much a value investor myself.

That means my portfolio is not very exciting. It is based on the fundamentals of the company or real estate or income instrument rather than on the story or the hype.

I guess you have gathered that I do not like Fluff. Quick traders can make money just by following the trends, but that is not my clients and that is not me. There is momentum investing and value investing. I am much better at value and longer term. When I need to fill that gap for one of my clients, I will get them the top outside manager that will handle that piece for us as a part of our allocation.

I do not, as many reports do, look at performance in three-year-period increments to judge the prowess of the manager. What I look at is the level of risk managers take and whether that has changed over the years.

These days, when a word from the media can affect the markets or a hideous act of terrorism can tank or make an entire economic sector, I also want to see how managers act during times of crisis or critical mass media coverage.

Does this person usually make changes, do they have a good sense of what is to come as demonstrated by their past behavior or do they get influenced by the media forecasts?

Notice I did not say past performance but past behavior. What can I expect? Some managers I expect to be erratic. Making change is their modus operandi. Others are noted for their consistency. I take notice when they become inconsistent.

In the last three years, there has been a flourishing of ETFs, Exchange Traded Funds.

ETFs are like indices, and they are affecting the individually managed accounts. I have no aversion to ETFs. The less expensive the client's fees, the better the bottom line. ETFs can be very cost-effective. But, like an index, I cannot offer hope of outperformance of the markets if I select only ETFs for your account, which by their nature reflect the market. But, I listen to the client. If they are perfectly happy with steady index performance, I will help them out.

Because my clients are people of means, sometimes extremely wealthy, their money has several agendas. We try for outperformance with some of their investments and go with the indices with others portions of their portfolio.

They also may have portfolios that they are managing for parents and children and for their business. Each has a separate purpose, a separate risk tolerance and, generally, a selection of different managers.

Before we leave this issue of management criteria, let me explain why I personally, and for my clients who want to beat the market, tend to stay away from very large funds. If you are managing $1 billion, you have to find a place for all that money. You might find a hidden gem with a smallish company. You might even buy it for yourself and wish you could invest for your clients.

But, each client would have such a small percentage of the company that it would make no real impact on their overall portfolio. As I once heard a manager say, "It is a good investment, but it doesn't pay for me to spend my time following it because it is simply too small."

If, like me, you like these hidden gems, you are going to want a manager with a reasonable amount under management instead of a mega-fund. I prize a manager who can be flexible when they see a good investment.

And it is not just about stocks. Take a short-term bond fund paying perhaps ½%. You may get charged more than what the bond yields in fees. You have just taken on a guaranteed loss. And you have a slight downside if rates go up. I am dumbfounded as to why anybody would go into a fund like that. They do. They think it is safe, that it's like a high yield money market fund; but, it is not. Or it could be that the fund was recommended in a different time and nobody reviewed the portfolio.

Take a client of mine I shall call Jaime. She had a substantial amount of money, actually millions, in one fund which she thought was a fund of short-term, two years or less, vehicles that yielded 1 ½%. What she never realized was that there was an internal fee of ½% plus the charge of

½% of which she was aware. Moreover, if short-term rates went up it could actually decimate her portfolio.

How could this happen?

Here I go again, but you must understand how the industry works to appreciate all The Fluff. This is a highly regulated industry. But, nobody stops you from buying lunch, having a seminar in a fancy room or making friends and relationships. In fact, that is necessary and encouraged.

People want to like, trust and get to know their financial advisor. So, we may accept losses and fail to ask questions because we have been befriended, we have gone to the annual events, we have read the brochure. The relationship makes us loyal and sometimes foolishly so.

I try as best I can to protect you from Fluff.

Here is my Modus Operandi:

- I look at managers every day.
- I track every trade.
- I research every industry.
- I change managers or look at changing when managers leave, or the firm merges with a bigger institution.
- I am patient. If a manager is underperforming for a while, I see what strategy they are using - maybe underperforming is part of their plan.
- I usually change managers when a new approach by a manager confounds my risk parameters, even if they will do well.

Ultimately, though, as a wealth manager, I am more than just a watcher of other managers. I am also the guide by your side.

For example, a client found a piece of real estate she wanted to buy and needed cash. A lot came into play. Is there a way to borrow at a very reasonable sum? If not, what should we select to liquidate? Many managers would simply keep the existing allocation and take some cash by liquidating equally from different parts of her portfolio.

I would take a deeper dive and consider when she planned to put the money back into the portfolio. If very soon, I might take it from an asset that I expected to go down in the future so she would be buying lower while selling higher. Logical.

It does take effort and time to make right decisions with foresight. If she never planned to put the money back, after choosing the investment to liquidate, I would rebalance her portfolio. And, that rebalancing would keep the integrity of our risk philosophy and be specific to her volatility parameters.

Is Rebalancing Bite or Bark?

What is rebalancing? On the simplest level, if someone has 50% in bonds and 50% in stocks, as their perfect allocation and stocks went up, the concept is that you would sell some stocks at a profit and buy bonds to keep the original allocation.

That is the knee-jerk way and sometimes such automation does not make sense.

Take the 529 college funds, for example. The closer your child gets to college age the more the risk is reduced. But, at today's low interest rates, long-duration bonds are just not going to cover the cost of a college education, particularly given the runaway inflation of tuition.

A ten-year duration bond gets you 1.8%. And if interest rates rise you could lose 10%. That is right, if interest rates go up from 1.8% to 2.8% tomorrow on a ten-year bond, your bond portfolio is down 10%. We do not rebalance for the sake of rebalancing.

I call this "KNEE-JERK rebalancing." The idea looks good in the 'gray brochure' – but an idea that is good for everybody is good for nobody.

We might not take profits from stocks right now unless people need capital for an exquisite opportunity. We have to look at things logically, not put our wealth on automatic pilot. If I am going to have a potential loss of 10% if interest rates go up, I want to have a potential gain worth the candle.

Right now, I am not calling the market. I think it has a potential to both go up and blow up. I am protecting the overall picture for some of my clients with dividend paying stocks, having some cash for opportunities I expect to arise, and investigating structured investments that are designed to be more aggressive than bonds but less aggressive than stocks. I look at options more than ever.

Risk analysis is more important than growth analysis.

While I understand it on a personal level, I really am amazed at how long intelligent people will stay with an advisor that is not performing. I was doing an analysis of a prospective client's portfolio, and he told me that he likes his advisor who has been working with him for over a decade. But, he lamented, "For some reason he is not getting any returns." I said, "You know, you can have the best genetically engineered seed; but if it is dropped on pavement, it is not going to grow."

Just like you, he looked bewildered. What can I possibly be talking about? I am speaking about the team as the fertile ground through which money can actually grow with consistency. His advisor had been lying back, making routine rebalancing of his portfolio along with many other clients. He was also using fund managers that ran very large funds with mediocre results. There was no real concerted effort to beat the market.

The goal was to have as little grief from the clients as possible and keep them on the books. Tax issues, succession planning, special opportunities, were all too much to be considered. There was no fertile soil in which to grow.

To understand what I mean by The Bite, take a look at investor behavior under a particular circumstance. When bond yields were high, everyone rushed into the bond market. Investors were buying all types of bonds with all types of maturity dates. There was also an appetite for investments that protected people against those rising Treasury rates.

Investors went to variable-rate bonds on the concept that they wanted to participate as rates rose and not lock in rates. They purchased senior floating rate notes. They gave up the security of a definite long-term return.

Corporations could borrow at a short-term low rate, LIBOR (the variable-rate plus 2% at that time). But, those borrowing rates were not locked in. If short-term rates went up, the LIBOR also went up, say another 2%. Now investors were getting LIBOR 2% plus 2% =4%. So, the higher the rates went, the more investors earned. They were protected from rising rates.

So far it sounds good, except for one simple thing. Most of these securities were very illiquid. This was an enormous debt market of $3 trillion; the bond market was bigger than the stock market.

Then greed came in. New types of notes were issued.

Vehicles were created like closed end, bond, mutual and hedge funds, all of which were stuck with these types of investments. So long as there was liquidity to pay, there was no issue. But, this chart shows the amount of outstanding corporate bonds.

Rough trade
The US corporate bond market

Outstanding corporate bonds, $trn / *Dealers' inventory of corporate bonds, $bn*

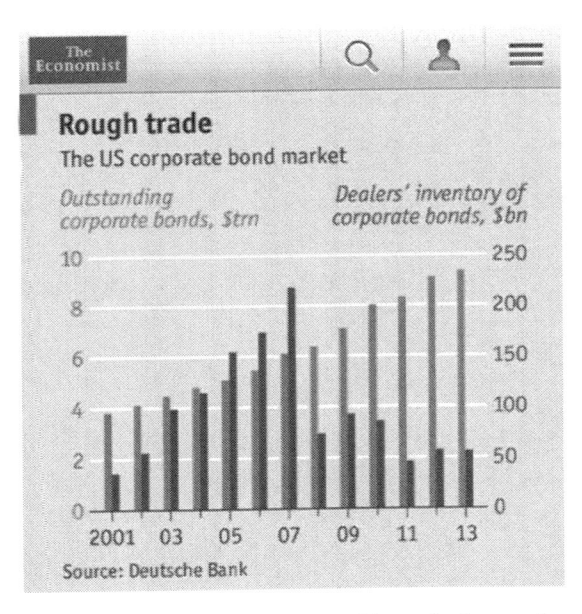

Source: Deutsche Bank

The chart shows that the amount of bonds issued were sky high; and the ability for any, even a large organization, to absorb those bonds now is dramatically less than in 2007. That could become our next liquidity crisis. Big supply, low demand. You know what happened in the past under similar circumstances. The value fell out, and people lost big.

Those were more than uncertain times. Those were crisis times. Dealers could not take on these securities. Frankly, it was a mess. In all of the many comments and writings about this crisis, the one factor that emerges is the creation of this liquidity problem.

Although this has not happened as yet, it will, in my opinion, if it is not fixed under the Dodd-Frank Wall Street Reform and Consumer Protection Act of 2010 or otherwise.

The intriguing part, and the terribly frightening part for today's investor, is that they might not even know they own illiquid debt securities, or that the liquidity problem exists.

With so many of these types of holdings in mutual funds and so few investors capable of looking at the exact holdings in a fund (Morning Star or your quarterly statements track the fund's performance as a whole), many investors will be taken by surprise.

You need to analyze your holdings so you know exactly what they are. It is not good enough to say that you are in a growth fund. What does the fund own? You cannot avoid it, and you will benefit if you know your holdings. Something is always waiting to happen.

Closed End Funds: Case in Point

Before the 2008 crisis, Closed End Funds, as discussed previously, were a darling of investors. Yet, very few understood what they are.

These funds own bonds like any bond fund, except that they accept only a certain amount of investors. They appear to be conservative. But, when they own illiquid high yield bonds with variable rates, the risk of default make such funds a higher risk investment.

What was most frightening was that most people owned these for the conservative portion of their portfolio. They considered the stock portion the risk. They never expected failure of their most conservative side.

That was a major reason for the panic. In 2008, CEFs were trading at a big discount to their net asset value. Sometimes you could buy into a CEF for as little as 80 cents on the dollar.

In turn, as people refused to take the risk, the bonds defaulted; and the net asset value of the funds went down. Net asset value is the actual amount each individual bond in the CEF is worth when added together. If every bond were sold as a separate bond, the seller would get more than the value of the total fund if every share were sold at market price.

A good analogy is a house sale. If you took the time to sell every piece of furniture, art, pot and pan individually, you would get a lot more than selling everything at once to a resale store owner. That store owner is getting a bargain. At one point, these closed end funds were down 30% to 40% from NAV. Actually, this became a huge buying opportunity. But, of course, by then, people were so frightened that they simply let it slide.

Now that was 2008, and this is TODAY.

Precisely while I was dictating this very paragraph, I noticed on the financial news, which is constantly playing on my big screen, that Bill Gross, founder of PIMCO, the largest bond fund, $270 billion in size, told a reporter, "There is no liquidity in the bond market currently."

Bill Gross made PIMCO the largest fund in the world; and, in turn, PIMCO was the biggest investor in the world. When this happened, Bill left. That made perfect sense and proves one of my points. The bond fund had become so large it became difficult to sell to anyone except within the fund.

Effectively, the growth created its own market and made it close to impossible for Gross to beat the market, which had been his stellar strong suit. What did the smartest investor in the world do? He started his own fund to buy what PIMCO sold. Gross went to the Janus Unconstrained Fund. It was a tiny fund when he took it over at $500 million of his own and $600 million from investors as of this date. He saw what the average investor could not see. When you have a big discount on a CEF, it is an opportunity for buying.

Currently, there are pretty nice discounts in CEFs. People are complacent at the moment. There is no doubt in my mind that we are going to have even greater discounts in this arena. And, yes, we could have a repeat of liquidity problems. Yet, people do need these types of investments. The smart thing to do is consider Exchange Traded Funds with short-term maturity date bonds. They are not going to be impacted nearly as much if rates go up, and you will get some yield. If and when there is a fallout, you have dry powder to re-allocate to those CEFs with a big discount.

Just see how logical this approach is. If CEFs are trading at a discount, most people just see what a bargain they are getting and jump in. But, now they are invested; and if there are defaults or simply rate changes, they will lose.

When that happens, those CEFs become real bargains; and it would be a great time to buy.

This buy low, sell high takes discipline. I wish you could see me right at this moment. I'm writing for you and to you. Simultaneously, I am watching four big TV screens. I never take my eyes off the market and the analysis. Frankly, I do very well in life and in my career. But you might not want to be me. I really am riveted by the screen feeding the logical information, the numbers of the analytics into every decision.

Now, I do not want anyone to panic. What if you are already in one of those closed end funds, and the liquidity is just not there? You have done your analysis of your portfolio, and you have a lot of holdings that might be at risk. Here again, you have got a go for The Bite not The Bark.

The Bark rears up when people become complacent. They are getting 6% in interest and dividends easily, and they compare it to a vehicle that has only 3% rate of return. So they fail to diversify. It is normal. We are all saying, "Why would I want 3% when I can get 6%?"

Ask yourself this, "Why are you getting 6% if US Treasuries are yielding 2 1/2%? What type of debt vehicle would give you more than twice what treasuries are yielding?"

There are only two answers.

Either you have longer-term bonds or you have high-risk bonds that pay a bigger spread (you might have both, longer-term bonds with higher risks). And, there is one more technical reason you may be getting more than a US Treasury.

CEFs use leverage. They borrow to buy bonds. If there is a problem, it will be even more amplified because of this debt hanging over the head of the funds. So, here we are with people exuberant over getting 6% because they do not understand the underlying disaster that could take place. If the CEF borrows at 1% and buys long-term bonds at 4%, the difference is profit. But, what happens when rates rise?

Closed end funds, too, usually use 30%-40% leverage. So, a portfolio of bonds which would usually go down 10% if rates rise, will now go down 13%-14% (3%-4% more) than if leverage had not been used.

The warning is simple. Figure out what you have and how sensitive your holdings are to interest rate rises. You have done well. You are not underwater. Do not panic. See how to take some of that risk out of your portfolio. When you are complacent, that is the time to see how much risk you have and get rid of the red flags.

It reminds me of 2007 and 2008 when people looked at the volatility in the mortgage market. There was barely any. So, they decided that they would simply leverage, borrow to buy. Instead of getting 4%, they were getting 15% and 16% by using leverage. They did not understand the risk that was building up. It was like a rubber band stretching, waiting to hit them in the face.

Other than hidden risk, there is another reason that most investors need expert help. They fail to take advantage of new opportunities that they see as risky and fear to enter until everybody else has done so, made money, and real moneymaking potential is over.

One such area is energy. Fracking has created multimillionaires. North Dakota has had a remarkable jump of 7.5% in millionaires between 2013-2015. We are going toward energy independence in spite of all the roadblocks that will be put in front of this industry. It is like having a massive tax cut for the entire economy when energy costs go down. We feel it at the pump, but it is magnified in benefits to big corporations. Because of energy savings, net earnings go up. There is more opportunity to grow. With oil prices below $30 per barrel, energy stocks and bonds are depressed. It is a terrific sector right now, and it is easy to invest in through an ETF in energy stocks.

All of our energy savings is going to translate into higher profits for corporations, more spending money for the average consumer, which is going to give the economy a pretty nice boost and, hopefully, create jobs.

I know this is beginning to sound like a prediction. I do not like predictions. Frankly, I want everything I put in writing to withstand the test of time. But, you must understand that with a good team, you really are not predicting. You are making a reasoned judgment.

In my first book, I did make one prediction: that US Treasuries were going to climb; and if you owned them, you would lose money. It did happen, and it is documented.

But, predictions are not what I rely upon for my decisions. We beat the market with a logical, consistent system. And I guarantee you one thing - you will not stick with that system unless you have trust in your advisor. You can only really trust an advisor if they deliver The Bite, not The Fluff or The Bark.

Chapter 14

Just The Bite

"This looks simple enough in the telling, and is merely the operation of Anselm Rothschild's famous advice, 'buy cheap and sell dear....' But when the statement is made that over 90% of public purchases are made at the approximate high tide of the market and about the same percentage of sales at the appropriate low tide, in short, that the most simple and reasonable methods of making money are not only disregarded, but actually reversed, a great field for analysis and discussion presents itself."

The Pitfalls of Speculation, by Thomas Gibson, The Moody Corporation, 1906

A cardiac stress test is used to measure the level of activity your heart can take before it becomes over-stressed.

This is not so different from a financial stress test to see if market activity will overwhelm your portfolio in the future (which might cause an actual heart attack).

To continue with the medical analogy, your investment stress test allows you to take precautions that might include surgery (buying or selling holdings), or at the very least, watching your holdings more carefully or more frequently than in the past.

By and large, we use an asset allocation model for our clients. As I mentioned in earlier Chapters, the asset classes you select can be more important over time to the overall performance of your portfolio than the individual assets you are holding. This is the teaching of economist Harry Markowitz, who conceived of what we call today **"Modern Portfolio Theory,"** for which he won the Nobel Prize.

We add logic to our decision making around our asset allocation mix by looking at the history of market performance over time. With our software (we use Bloomberg), we can check portfolios against hundreds of variables and see what would happen under an almost unlimited number of circumstances. We can replicate how the portfolio would have fared under both stark market conditions or in a go-go market environment. Changing these variables and seeing the outcomes we call "the stress test."

For example, bring yourself back to 1987 with a portfolio half in stocks and half in government bonds. The stock market dropped by 22%. Bonds appreciated in value by 8%. Because you are 50% in the market, your portfolio has a negative performance of 7%. (50% of the account goes down 22% so you lose 11% in stocks, but 50% of your portfolio that is in bonds has gone up 8%, so the contribution from bonds is .5x .08=.04, or a positive 4%. Negative 11% from stocks plus positive 4% from bonds equals a net loss of 7%, during the time you had the 50/50 split.)

Let us say that the other half of your portfolio in government securities goes up 3%. A stress test will show you, with much more detail, what the actual outcome would be with your current portfolio during times of market stress and compare that with the outcome if you had a different asset allocation of the same assets or a different set of asset classes.

We can change variables with stocks, bonds and also commodities, currencies and any trackable investment asset.

How stressed your portfolio would be under past market circumstances is just the beginning of what you need to know to see if the current mix is right for you. We can stress test into the future and see what would happen to your portfolio if:

- Interest rates drop
- Inflation rates rise or fall
- There are changes in third world markets
- There is trouble on foreign exchanges

And more.

We can also stress test where your portfolio is sensitive under macroeconomic conditions. For example, is your portfolio subject to sensitivity when the unemployment rate rises? In fact, a stress test is exactly what the government gave the big banks by looking at their balance sheets, to see how sensitive they were to certain conditions before determining a bailout.

But, the beauty of our stress test is that it goes beyond analytics.

There is a secondary game plan that we can use if a negative scenario takes place. We know your comfort zone in advance so we can move with speed and confidence.

This is the complex issue of human nature - how stressed you would be as a human being if you had losses of varying calibers. This relates back to our discussion of behavioral finance in Part II of this book. We want you to have backup, just like an aircraft carrier can deploy artillery, but the Marines can also land and fight on the ground.

Why do we care about your feelings as to the strain a stressed-out portfolio would cause? Do feelings affect market performance?

They sure do. In *What Works on Wall Street*, and other of his writings, Mr. O'Shaughnessy reminds us that, although, we often start with an investment system in which we believe, we just as often lose fortunes by not sticking to it. He points out that the human tendency toward self-distrust is as pervasive with the guys on Wall Street, like money managers

Celebrating O'Shaughnessy's Book Signing with Mary, James, Jimmy & Wayne

and fund managers, as it is with the average guy on any street.

When managers of funds buy and sell on "the next big thing" and stray from their tested program, millions of shares are bought or sold and the market is affected. Studies show that the straying is more often caused by some emotional decision on their part, like not wanting to be left out of tech stocks, or looking bad for a time while a sector that they are invested in takes a temporary loss.

Yes, we must take account of the stress that creates YOUR abandonment of the strategy too soon, or failure to execute too late.

Is there such a thing as a totally stress-free portfolio?

No. Even cash under a mattress can lose buying power if inflation goes up, or our currency is devalued against other currencies. The cash in your pocket may still be $50, but it buys only $25 worth of goods and services.

How about money market funds, are they Steady Eddie?

Not necessarily.

Even money-market funds fluctuate in value; in fact, the net asset value (the total value of the bonds in the fund divided by the number of units outstanding) fluctuates daily. But, they are "agreed" to trade at a steady $1 per share, so you are protected. There is talk about revealing the actual value of underlying assets.

Money-market funds invest in short-term paper. The SEC requires holdings to mature in 90 days or less. Treasuries may go out two years, and commercial paper one year, but the average maturity must be 90.

The paper owned in tax-free money funds is exactly what you would buy for yourself if you were looking for low risk, with respectable returns:

- Tax anticipation notes

- Bond anticipation notes

- Commercial paper from tax-exempt issuers, like municipal hospitals and port authorities

Recently, funds have been created that hold paper issued by one state exclusively.

Money-market funds may appear to be identical. Indeed, one of their virtues is that they are close enough in return (50 basis points or so) not to give you analysis paralysis in selecting an account. But, to the connoisseur, they are not identical.

There are the super-safe varieties, which hold only US Treasuries and are consequently state tax-free. There are those touting yield, which invest in commercial paper to slightly spruce up returns. For those seeking backup insurance for their funds, cash management accounts offered by brokerage houses are SIPC insured from between $100,000 to $5,000,000. Bank funds are insured through FDIC. However, they may offer several basis points less than mutual funds or brokerage money markets, and generally do not offer tax-free accounts.

Wow, all these significant differences just in looking at money-market funds. Imagine the complexity in stress testing an allocated portfolio with investments like stocks, or corporate bonds. Well, it is really not so hard. And, in the next Chapter we will analyze several real scenarios.

Chapter 15

The Relationship of Asset Allocations

to Your Goals

"An examination of almost four thousand speculative accounts, extending over a period of ten years, developed results interesting and instructive in many ways. The examination was other an exhaustive character, and covert operations of every conceivable nature in both stocks and cereals. In these accounts all the errors of speculation were distinctly illustrated. The three principal points developed by the investigation were that 80% of the accounts showed a final loss; that the tendency to buy at the top and sell at the bottom was most prevalent; and that most of the operations appeared to be of a purely gambling character. The further fact was established that successes almost invariably lead to excesses."

> The Pitfalls of Speculation, by Thomas Gibson, The Moody Corporation, 1906

You might like to see some standard asset allocation scenarios. Do not adopt them for yourself, as one size certainly does not fit all. Here are a few. Then we will take steps to customize an asset allocation for you.

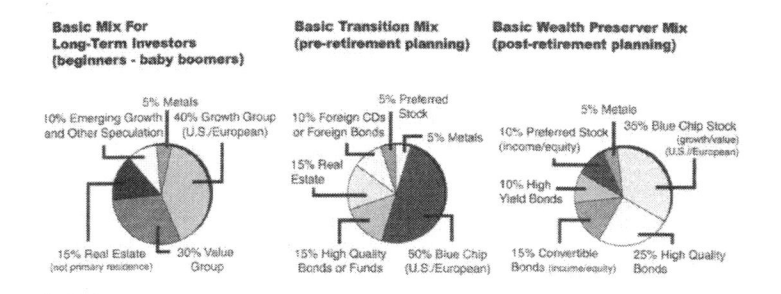

Basic Mix For Long-Term Investors (beginners - baby boomers)
- 5% Metals
- 10% Emerging Growth and Other Speculation
- 40% Growth Group (U.S./European)
- 15% Real Estate (not primary residence)
- 30% Value Group

Basic Transition Mix (pre-retirement planning)
- 5% Preferred Stock
- 10% Foreign CDs or Foreign Bonds
- 5% Metals
- 15% Real Estate
- 15% High Quality Bonds or Funds
- 50% Blue Chip (U.S./European)

Basic Wealth Preserver Mix (post-retirement planning)
- 5% Metals
- 10% Preferred Stock (income/equity)
- 10% High Yield Bonds
- 15% Convertible Bonds (income/equity)
- 25% High Quality Bonds
- 35% Blue Chip Stock (growth/value) (U.S./European)

So, with a well worked out allocation, what can one expect in actual bottom line dollars and sense/cents? Below is a chart, simplified but displaying the retirement prospects of an actual client. It looks pretty good:

Beginning Portfolio Value: $1,500,000

Goals: Annual Retirement Needs: $100,000

Assumptions: Inflation: 2%

Portfolio: 35% Stock

Projected Return: 7.42%

Standard Deviation: 7.79

Age	Year	Portfolio Value	Soc. Sec. Earnings	Investment Income	Taxes	Goals Retirement	Travel	Ending Value
65	2012	1500000	0	111,300	22,260	0	0	1,589,040
66	2013	1,589,040	0	117,907	23,581	-	0	1,683,365
67	2014	1,683,365	30,268	124,906	31,035	100,000	10,000	1,697,504
68	2015	1,697,504	30,873	125,955	31,366	102,000	10,200	1,710,767
69	2016	1,710,767	31,491	126,939	31,686	104,040	10,404	1,723,067
70	2017	1,723,067	32,121	127,852	31,994	106,121	10,612	1,734,312
71	2018	1,734,312	32,763	128,686	32,290	108,243	10,824	1,744,403
72	2019	1,744,403	33,418	129,435	32,571	110,408	11,041	1,753,237
73	2020	1,753,237	34,087	130,090	32,835	112,616	11,262	1,760,700
74	2021	1,760,700	34,768	130,644	33,082	114,869	11,487	1,766,675
75	2022	1,766,675	35,464	131,087	33,310	117,166	11,717	1,771,033
76	2023	1,771,033	36,173	131,411	33,517	119,509	11,951	1,773,640
77	2024	1,773,640	36,897	131,604	33,700	121,899	12,190	1,774,351
78	2025	1,774,351	37,634	131,657	33,858	124,337	12,434	1,773,013
79	2026	1,773,013	38,387	131,558	33,989	126,824	12,682	1,769,462
80	2027	1,769,462	39,155	131,294	34,090	129,361	12,936	1,763,525
81	2028	1,763,525	39,938	130,854	34,158	131,948	13,195	1,755,015
82	2029	1,755,015	40,737	130,222	34,192	134,587	13,459	1,743,737
83	2030	1,743,737	41,551	129,385	34,187	137,279	13,728	1,729,480
84	2031	1,729,480	42,383	128,327	34,142	140,024	14,002	1,712,021
85	2032	1,712,021	43,230	127,032	34,052	142,825	14,282	1,691,124
86	2033	1,691,124	44,095	125,481	33,915	145,681	14,568	1,666,535
87	2034	1,666,535	44,977	123,657	33,727	148,595	14,859	1,637,988
88	2035	1,637,988	45,876	121,539	33,483	151,567	15,157	1,605,197
89	2036	1,605,197	46,794	119,106	33,180	154,598	15,460	1,567,858
90	2037	1,567,858	47,730	116,335	32,813	157,690	15,769	1,525,651

In taking the first step in creating your mix, we start with several questions, some of which you have answered in earlier Chapters, do not get overwhelmed. You have done half the work already.

We ask these questions (and more) in our Client Profile/Discovery Meeting.

Values:

- What does money mean to your life?

Goals:

- What are your top accomplishments? What would you like them to be?
- What are your personal goals?
- What are your professional goals?
- What do you do (or want to do) for your children?
- What do you do (or want to do) for your parents?
- Ideally, where would you like to be when you are 45? 55? 65? 75?
- What are your material quality of life desires (houses, travel, boats, or cars)?

Relationships:

- Which family member relationships (spouse, children, siblings, parents, etc.) are the most important ones to you?

Assets:

- What is your source of income (privately held business, employer, or professional compensation)?
- What benefits do you get from your workplace?
- What life insurance do you have?
- What property do you have (real property, artwork, jewelry)?
- How are your assets structured now (sole ownership, joint, corporate ownership, LLC, partnership, etc.)?
- What new assets do you expect to receive (for example, from inheritances or stock options)?
- How often do you want an overall review of your financial situation and progress toward your goals?
- Who else do you want involved in the management of your finances (spouse, other advisors such as an accountant or an attorney)?

We do need to know your hopes and dreams, likes and dislikes, your goals and timelines. This might seem "touchy-feely" to you. So, let me give you the "suit analogy," which I hope will work to make it clear. You can have a wonderfully tailored business suit, but what if you really needed a bathing suit? It just would not work for your purpose, and you would still be out there trying to find a bathing suit. That is what happens to moneymaking allocations when the purpose is off. If you have all your money in income and you are a new father with a good job, you will soon abandon the perfect income portfolio as you need growth and access to principle at times.

How can you help your advisor determine the rate of return you need?

First, determine the goal and a time when you want to reach the goal. The usual example is retirement. In order for you to determine the rate of return you will need to meet *retirement* goals, you must come to grips with three factors: (1) from where your retirement income will come, (2) when you will receive your retirement income, and (3) how much income you will receive.

Here are some useful tools to help you focus.

I. *From where will your retirement income come?*

List your sources of retirement income.

II. *When will these retirement resources be available to you?*

Once you know from where your retirement income will come, determine when it will be available. For some items, like Social Security, you can choose a date after age 62. In others, like pensions, you may have a choice. In yet other areas, like inheritance, you must guess. If you own your business, you can manage the timing of the sale. Do your best to work out the year in which most of what you plan to live on after retirement is available to you.

And by the way, let us get rid of phrases like "early retirement." "Early" compared to what? Because Social Security used to kick in at age 65, and many companies simply gave you a gold watch when you reached that age, it is still arbitrarily used. We want to know when you can retire, as much as we want to know when you would like to retire.

III. *How much money will you need to live on when you retire?*

Knowing how much and when you will receive money that is not dependent on your labor, gives you a better idea of your retirement target date. But, there is more. To actually be able to retire, your income must meet your expenses. If your retirement income falls short of retirement outflow, you must either wait or save more, plan to work or reduce costs.

There will be complex questions that will arise:

- Should you take an early retirement and withdraw under an IRS approved plan from your qualified plans before age 59 1/2?
- Should you retire and enhance your lifestyle with penalty-free withdrawals from your qualified plans, after age 59 ½?
- Should you take early Social Security?
- Should you take Social Security at the usual age or wait until 70?
- Should you start a second career and continue or start taking Social Security?
- What is the best pension withdrawal strategy?
- A large number of my corporate executive clients have stock options. How to manage those is always an important aspect of their retirement planning.

Stock Option Options

Do you own a Piece of Your Company? Stock Options and Restricted Stock?

Stock options and, to some extent, restricted stocks are a low-cost way for your employer to provide you with extra compensation while increasing incentive to produce for the company. A stock option gives the employee the right to buy stock in the company at a given price (the "strike price") for a given time (the "exercise period," typically up to 10 years). Restricted stocks are shares in your company that only become yours after a vesting period.

Restricted stock options are more like salary and do reduce a company's bottom line but are attractive because their cost, unlike cash bonuses, can be spread out over the vesting period.

Stock options cost your employer less to offer than an immediate bonus or raise. They do not reduce your company's bottom line and can, if stock prices rise, actually provide the company with tax deductions without cash outlay. (The employer can deduct the difference between the price of the option when given and the price when exercised.)

Here is how it works: your employer grants you an option to buy 1000 shares of your company for $40. The stock is currently selling for $45. You can exercise your option and immediately sell the shares. You have a $5,000 gain; your company has a $5,000 deduction.

Or, you can hold on to your option while your company grows and its stock price keeps going up. It costs you nothing to wait; and in 5 years, when the share price is $88, you can exercise your option at $40 and immediately sell the stock for $88, pocketing $48,000.

Cash Flow and Tax Consequences of Exercising Options

Once you have been offered a stock option, you have three choices:

1. The No Cash Turnover (either now or later) - You do not have to actually pay for the shares when you exercise the option. If you simultaneously sell the

shares you buy on the option, your broker will offset one against the other and you will receive only the difference (less commission, of course). You can do this at any time before the option expires.

2. Exercise the Option, Now - This will actually cost you money. You must buy the stock at the option price. Then, hold on to the stock and sell it as you would any other investment.

3. Exercise the Option, Later - Again, this will cost you the same amount as if you did not wait, but you pay at a later date. So, why wait? Answer: To see if the price of the shares goes up. There is no risk to waiting; the cost to you is the same.

There are tax consequences to each of these transactions, both as ordinary income and capital gains. You will have to pay taxes on ordinary income when you exercise the option. (Provided that there is no "qualified plan" involved.) (These have their own tax rules.) The tax is figured on the difference between the market value and the exercise price on the date you actually exercise the option. You will also pay the reduced capital gains tax on the difference between the market price on the date of option exercise and the price you eventual sell price.

A Good Compromise Choice

The Solution: Dollar Cost Averaging - If you are having a problem deciding when and how to exercise your options, do it on a schedule. Exercise a fixed portion of your options at fixed intervals. In this way, you spread out your risk and your tax burdens.

Objective Numbers for a Subjective Investment Factor

Now we have a good idea of how much recurring income you will have at retirement, like Social Security and a pension;

and we figure in your stock options, if any. We know how much investment capital you have to invest and how much cash flow you need. We can see the shortfall - the difference between the cash flow you need and what you will have.

So Far, So Good

Now, with all this personal assessment, we can figure out the ideal Rate of Return, ROR, you need to live the life you love after retirement. But, there is another question to answer beyond this. What risk are you willing to take to achieve that ROR?

"Risk" is more than a state of mind. It is not a subjective feeling or an instinct, although it certainly seems that way most of the time. A "risky" investment is not one that you are afraid to go into because you may lose money. That can and does happen with even the safest (or seemingly safest) investments. If you do not think so, look at the market value of your Treasury Bills. While these investments are absolutely secure at maturity when you are guaranteed the recovery of your principle, they are not so risk free while you are holding them. Values rise and fall as interest rates fall and rise. And those changes can be steep. That is Risk.

Risk for investors is, rather, an objective measure of an investment's volatility.

It is the degree to which the market value of the investment fluctuates. Risk is measured by mathematical calculation, probability and statistical analysis. Risk is also a comparative measurement, setting the volatility of one investment against that of another or against a standard. To understand risk, therefore, you must measure volatility LOGICALLY.

Standard Deviation

The primary measurement of volatility and risk is standard deviation. This measurement is as old as the science of statistics itself. (It was first used in the early 1700's.) It measures the degree to which individual occurrences, in this case, stock prices, deviate from the average. Think of it as making the concept of "average" more meaningful. (Weather is a good analogy....a day in which the average temperature was 50 degrees because the high was 55 and the low was 45 is not the same weather day as one in which the average temperature was also 50, but the high was 100 and the low 0 degrees.)

Standard deviation in investments measures the likely price range based on the movement of prices over and above the average price. Usually, it measures the movement over and under a 3-year average. The formula is complicated, but it arrives at a number within which there is a 68% chance of the stock price falling over or above the average. And twice that number, or two standard deviations, reflects the price range 95% of the time. If a stock has an average price of 50 and a standard deviation of 15, it means that 68% of the time the price of the stock was between 35 and 65 (50 plus or minus 15) and 95% of the time the price was between 20 and 80 (50 plus or minus 30, or two standard deviations). The higher the standard deviation is, the more volatile the stock; therefore, the more risky.

Beta is Better

As useful as standard deviation is (see our 'doggy' example) in measuring risk, there is an even more precise measure. Developed by Nobel Prize winning economist, William Sharpe, in the 1960's, Beta measures standard deviation relative to a benchmark index, usually the S&P 500. It is simpler and easier to understand.

What Beta calculation does is plot the plus and minus price change of the stock or fund being examined and the plus and minus price change of the index and then measures the "slope" of the line created. (Remember your high school math?) This gives the Beta of the examined stock.

The higher the Beta, the more volatile the stock.

A stock with a Beta of 1, for example, has moved in lockstep with the index and is expected to do that in the future. A stock with a Beta of 1.5 has and probably will move 50% more than the S&P 500. That is, if the S&P rises by 10%, the stock with a Beta of 1.5 should rise 15%; and if the S&P falls 20%, it will fall by 30%. It is more volatile, and more risky. Likewise, a stock with a Beta of .75 will rise only 7.5% when the S&P goes up 10%, but will fall only 15% when the S&P drops by 20%. It is less volatile and thus less risky.

So you can see how the risk calculation fits into the ROR calculation. But, there is more to it. If a manager touts his or her results with high Beta stocks without your understanding risk, you are being handed 'Fluff.' If they say they made more than the market and the market just happened to be up, you are hearing 'Bark.' Consistent performance with commensurate risk is 'Bite.'

We put these calculations of risk and return together with the choices you have in retirement, to come up with the right rate of return for you. That is what we will tackle in the next Chapter.

Chapter 16

Finding the Rate of Return of an Investment

For most planning goals and the asset allocation to fulfill them, we judge our portfolio by the rate of return we receive.

We make decisions and hope for the best rate with the least risk we can get. But, when we invest logically, it is not that haphazard. We calculate rather than guess. You are about to discover several calculations methods to determine rate of return.

No, you won't have to do them.

They are presented to show you how logic and mathematics can take the stress off you and your portfolio, and how an understandable calculation can make you more secure and less apt to make unnecessary changes and deviate from a good program. Think of this as a "feel good" session with numbers.

Rate of Return in a Nutshell

- Is the level of risk logical for the risk you are taking, considering the return you are getting?
- Could you get the same return for less risk elsewhere?
- Could you get a higher return for the same risk elsewhere?
- Could you get a higher return for less risk elsewhere?

Investopedia, one of the best websites on financial literacy, says the following about rate of return:

Definition of 'Rate Of Return'

The gain or loss on an investment over a specified period, expressed as a percentage increase over the initial investment cost.

Gains on investments are considered to be any income received from the security plus realized capital gains.

A rate of return measurement can be used to measure virtually any investment vehicle, from real estate to bonds and stocks to fine art, provided the asset is purchased at one point in time and then can be evaluated against the original purchase price at some time in the future.

If you want to learn more of the technical aspects of rate of return visit: www.investopedia.com

When we work with rate of return, we see what your portfolio must return to meet your needs; and we back out taxes and inflation to arrive at an accurate rate. The challenge is to be accurate in determining whether the investments we have selected will provide that rate: the required rate of return.

Required Rate of Return is defined as:

"a component in many of the metrics and calculations used in corporate finance and equity valuation. It goes beyond just identifying the return of the investment, and factors in risk as one of the key considerations to determining potential return. The required rate of return also sets the minimum return an investor should accept, given all other options available and the capital structure of the firm."

To calculate the required rate, you must look at factors such as the return of the market as a whole, the rate you could get if you took on no risk (the risk-free rate of return), and the volatility of the stock or the overall cost of funding the project. Here we examine this metric in detail and show you how to use it to calculate the potential returns of your investments.

Investopedia has published an illuminating and mathematically intense article by Peter Cherewyk, **How To Calculate Required Rate Of Return,** which reviews how to calculate the Required Rate of Return for different purposes, from which the foregoing is taken. Mr. Cherewyk's article is well worth reading; find it at: *www.investopedia.com/articles/fundamental-analysis/11/calculating-required-rate-of-return.asp#ixzz1vc6tb1oX*

What I can assure you about this important metric is that we, at The Moldaver Group, can always calculate the real and required rate of return for you. It is the assumptions that we use to make the calculation that can vary a bit from client to client. What you need is the assumptions to be tailored for you. I will address this in the next Chapter.

Chapter 17

How to Pick a Rate of Return

That is Right for You

Next in importance to the suicidal tendency to sell cheap and by dear was the widespread evidence of greed. In almost every case where an account was successfully begun, the operations were immediately extended in volume until, even after a large number of successful results, a single reverse wiped out the entire credit. ...The inability of the average trader to map out a plan and follow it was also distinctly exemplified."

The Pitfalls of Speculation, by Thomas Gibson, The Moody Corporation, 1906

In today's low interest rate environment getting a high rate of return is quite a trick. For anyone who is using his or her assets in retirement or to create a cash flow in any way, there is no such thing as a risk-free rate of return today. Yes, you may have enjoyed 8% in the past on your Treasuries and may again in the future. Some of our selected fund managers get returns in the teens, even today. But, those results are unpredictable.

What is logical is to be realistic and see how an income portfolio might fare over the next five years. If it is impossible to achieve the rate of return that you need, we can always look at hedge funds that beat the indices and can be "opportunistic."

Yes, there are some investments that can get 20% to 30% using opportunistic money, but they cannot be duplicated over any length of time with any guarantees.

If you are committed to earning a predictable interest rate in a low-interest rate environment, we need to include corporate bonds, foreign bonds, dividend paying stocks, and notes, and perhaps real estate investment trusts, REITs.

Currently, we are looking at floating rate securities with an acceptable credit risk. These days, we are shopping hard to ferret out issues that have an acceptable risk to return combination.

Once again, reality dictates what is logical. If you cannot take a bigger risk and you need a higher return, you may be forced to lower your spending or postpone spending. This is where an advisor works with you not just on your portfolios, but also on your life goals and personal characteristics.

Do not despair.

Especially in bad times, there are great buys out there for those that are not swayed by the media. Let us take this homey analogy and see if it sounds familiar. Let us say that in your neighborhood, there is a well-run bagel shop, a $4-a-cup coffee shop and a burger drive-through. They are all run by solid family members who contribute to their community, and you have fun patronizing these establishments. Now you read that there were riots in the streets of Greece, and the economy is taking a plunge here and abroad. Would you stop buying your bagel and morning coffee and burger lunch? Mostly, you'd continue those activities.

Now, let us pretend that those shops were actually companies listed on the stock exchange and the value of their stock plummeted, having nothing to do with the economics and earnings of their company. This is when you buy. Look at the company, not at the irrelevant factors that are affecting its price in the market. Know what you own and why you own it.

That is how inefficient markets help us buy low and sell high. What a concept! And that is how you can increase the return on your portfolio, even in the lowest of interest rate environment.

Forget the minute-to-minute news and look at company specific characteristics like price earnings ratios, sales, and price momentum – in short, follow the stock.

My favorite pundit, James P. O'Shaughnessy, whom I have mentioned to you in prior Chapters, bought Apple at $18 a share because it was priced at two times sales, not at 20 times sales with a sexy story. The stock eventually split at $700 a share.

I believe in using experts. In fact, with all my knowledge, I still use expert managers who have very deep and specific knowledge in different areas of investing. That is one reason I covered money market funds in the Chapter on Stress Testing a portfolio, to show you how much knowledge is needed to make a logical decision about a seemingly simple aspect of investing.

Yes, I know you want to learn how to "pick" stocks in today's low interest rate environment, especially if you have a shortfall in your goals. You are about to discover one way of how to do this in detail (there are many protocols for stock picking, but I will show you the "Simple Simon Way").

Even so, I cannot emphasize enough that you must work with an advisor. There is no way to have the access to a broad variety of investments working alone or even through an investing group or club. Nevertheless, it is worth your understanding some of the details of investment selection because it will help you access the prowess of your advisor or financial professional.

How to Do a Simple Simon Stock Search

A stock search is merely a look at all stocks that meet certain criteria. When you have isolated a list of stocks that meet those criteria, you make the list of requirements more stringent until you have only a few candidates to consider buying. If you already have a hunch, tip, idea or recommendation of a stock, you can use the same criteria to see if that stock would qualify to be included in the search.

Stock analysts have identified over 200 criteria that indicate whether a stock will make money in the future, how fast and how much. The factors carry different weight. For example, the age of the CEO is of much less weight than the past and projected earnings for the company.

Computer programs differ by the amount of factors you can apply in your search and the weight they give them. Some programs allow you to weight the factors yourself, others have them adjustable and others build them in.

With computer software search tools, Warren Buffet and you have the same information available.

How to Narrow the Universe of Thousands Available Stocks and Pick a Winner

Now, remember what you are looking for. You want a stock that will grow in value or pay high dividends. Here is where investors go wrong. They try to pick a stock based on what is hot or in the news. We do the opposite. Our decision making does not entail actively selecting the best stock. Our investment decision making entails actively rejecting the wrong stocks until there is only one left from which to choose. Think of it as a monumental game of "Simon Says."

The Stock Left Standing, Wins.

To remain standing, a stock must meet more of the following criteria than other competing stocks:

- **Substantial Insider Buying** - Use 3-month net insider buying to determine whether insider buying is high. Net insider buying is the number of shares bought by insiders in the company, over the past three months, minus the number of shares sold by them. The extent of insider trading must be reported to the SEC, and the information is readily available. Look for stocks where at least 20% of the company's insiders are buying. That's why the best rule is to buy companies that are still controlled by their billionaire founders.

- **Be Undervalued** - Stocks with good past and current growth that are slated by analysts for future growth over the next five years but priced low compared to the stock's long-term price trend, are dubbed **undervalued**. In other words, the stock is selling for less than it is worth. To find and follow an undervalued stock, you need to know its price over a period of time (I use five years, more conservative pickers will insist on a ten-year look).

- **Display Accelerated Growth (Momentum)** - A stock with "momentum" is one that is not only growing in price but also growing incrementally. (The growth was greater in each period than in the period before.) Expressed mathematically, **Momentum = Rate of Change in Stock Prices, Over Time.** With the help of the computer, you can gauge momentum for industry groups, insider trading, price to earnings ratio (P/E) and many other useful indicators.

- **Momentum can be tracked for stock prices,** company earnings and industry group growth. Let us say you want only those stocks 1) whose price is increasing faster than 90% of all other stocks, 2) in an industry group that is growing more than 90% faster than all other industries, and 3) whose earnings are growing faster than 90% of all other stock in that industry. A search can limit your universe to just those high flyers. You then eliminate from your universe those stocks that meet the criteria, but which have just started to decrease in momentum.

- Once you have narrowed stocks by P/E, insider transactions and value or momentum, apply these three criteria:

- **Is a favorite of Institutional Investors?** - Institutional investors often put a floor on a stock (a price at which they will always buy the stock), or a ceiling (a price at which they will always sell). These floors and ceilings, called support and resistance levels, will be important in deciding when to buy and sell. A stock that boasts levels bolstered by institutional buyers is much easier to trade because the floors and ceilings are easier to track with precision.

- **Does it display Positive Cash Flow?** - The **Accumulation/Distribution Index** allows you to follow the money, usually to confirm institutional trading. You track whether on up days the volume of trading is greater than on down days. This tells you if money is flowing into or away from a heavily traded stock.

- **Does it rate well with Wall Street Analysts (Particularly in the area of Projected Earnings)?** - Look for a stock followed by several analysts to get a greater depth of research. Focus on the one-month change in earnings estimates both before and after you buy.

> **Look Again Before You Buy**
>
> Once you have finished your search, you still probably have too many stocks still standing in your SIMON SAYS game. To eliminate more, simply add more factors to your search. Here is where judgment comes in. Here are the factors ranked solely on the basis of my experience and priorities.
>
> - Debt to equity
> - Earnings
> - Dividends paid not from borrowing but from real profits
> - Cash in the company
> - Earnings momentum against all other companies in the sector
>
> 5-30 day average volume indicator shows institutional interest in a stock by comparing trading volume over the past 5 days with the past 30 days. "Hot Stocks" show a marked increase in recent institutional trading.

Narrowing the Universe by Sector

Once you are ready to focus on a stock category (i.e., large-cap, small-cap, foreign) further narrow the universe by concentrating on the sector of the economy that you believe will have the best growth potential. Trackers and indices like Dow and S&P create the business sectors. Mutual funds have expanded them. Today computer programs follow anywhere from 75-200 business categories or sectors. Trends within sectors are set by big money pension funds, bankers and other institutional investors.

With our computer as a tool, this logical look at "hot" sectors can be confirmed or denied with concrete facts and analysis. "New Economy" stocks like hi-tech, biotech and telecommunication can be singled out. How? In the same way that you do stock searches, you can do a stock sector search. In fact, sector searches are easier than individual stock searches. You can then select a fund or limit your stock search only to industries in this sector. You can also research the sector to see if it is falling into disfavor as a sell indicator and reposition stocks into another sector.

ETFs can help with sector investing. They cover entire sectors and are less expensive than many sector mutual funds. They are no match for expertise that beats the market, but ETFs help the less initiated do better. Diversification is a protection against ignorance (the ignorance of what will happen next in the market), and there is nothing wrong with that.

Narrowing the Universe by Cost

A more expensive stock can tie up too much cash. But, low price stocks may be over the counter and thinly traded or have few analysts following them.

Once you have found the right stock, fund, manager and sector, you need to be sure it fits in with your asset allocation model. In the next Chapter, let us bring everything together the logical way. We will see that diversification is a protection against ignorance. And there is nothing wrong with that.

The Team Ringing the New York Stock Exchange Bell
With Mary Sliwa, James Lee, Wayne Chrebet, Mike Von Borsig, and Mary Bennett

Chapter 18

Asset Allocation to Improve The Bite

"The tip may be briefly described as illogical. In considering this statement the dividing line between tips and information must be clearly drawn, for one is frequently found masquerading in the habit of the other."

The Pitfalls of Speculation, by Thomas Gibson, The Moody Corporation, 1906

I have taken more all of these pages to make these essential points:

- Know your goal.

- See if the rate of return you are getting will fulfill that goal.

- If not, choose a winning allocation by doing extensive computer testing of the probabilities that the allocation will work for you.

- Choose the stocks and other assets that will fill the allocation.

- Do not be persuaded by the latest news in sticking to the allocation.

- Stress test the portfolio to see what happens if the market changes - can you take it. If you can, the day-to-day news won't bother you. But, you must be able to avoid the temptation to follow the herd.

Maybe you are thinking, "Boy, that sounds too easy." All I can say is this; it is not easy, but it is simple.

There are logical steps in making an asset allocation:

- Choose asset classes (large-cap, small-cap, international, emerging markets, bonds, cash, commodities, physical gold, value and more)
- Select the percentage of your portfolio that each asset class will occupy
- Select the individual investments within each asset class
- Rebalance

Rebalancing is done under four circumstances:

1. When one asset class does so well that the percentage that it occupies in your portfolio is greater than the original allocation, sell and take a profit.

2. When one asset class sinks below the percentage of your portfolio that it was intended to occupy, buy more.

3. When there are adjustments in the risk that you wish to take or the goals that you wish to achieve, rethink the allocation.

4. When you become enamored with an asset class that you have left out of your portfolio in the past, like gold, real estate, or commodities depending on the market, and they fit into the original rate of return goal with a risk you can tolerate, find room for them in the allocation.

Within each asset class, you might want to change your holdings because you have become wealthier and can now "afford" investments that were out of your reach, like hedge funds, limited partnerships, or some other type of alternative investment you have encountered in your investment journey.

As you build wealth, you still must access risk and never illogically overburden your portfolio with fast-track, high-loss exposure investments. Luckily, as we have seen in earlier Chapters, because of the computer and the input of a few economic and mathematical geniuses, we can analyze an allocation and the investments in it for risk.

Economist Harry Markowitz determined that portfolio risk was as important as portfolio return. A portfolio is efficient, and logicians like us want an efficient portfolio when it yields comparable results with less risk or better results with the same or less risk as competing portfolio choices. To decrease risk, you buy across different sectors, industries, and asset classes. This is quite different from the advice of the famous pundit, Bernard Baruch, who stated, "Put all your eggs in one basket, and watch that basket."

That was an old way of thinking when there were few stocks and fewer choices in any other asset class. Perhaps that is why Harry's way is called, MODERN Portfolio Theory.

Modern thinking in investment portfolio allocation structure, to lower risk and preserve rate of return, did not stop with Harry. In fact, asset allocation by modern portfolio rules is just the starting point. Today asset classes do not correlate as they did in decades past, with one class going down as the other rises.

Take another look at the above graphic.

Often asset classes rise at the same time, but at different rates. That is why we stress test with more than just the asset class and concentrate much more on the assets in each allocation than in the past. That is also why asset allocated routine mutual funds are not delivering as they used to. You probably know that from your own portfolio performance in the past several years.

In conducting a stress test of your portfolio, take a tip from another pundit, a mathematician from the Harvard Business School, Jack Treynor. He might not be as familiar to investors as Harry Markowitz, but Treynor devised a formula known as the Treynor Ratio with the goal of rating the management of investment funds.

We can rate your portfolio through the Treynor Ratio, as well. The formula takes a portfolio's total return and subtracts a risk-free rate of return, like a Treasury bill yield. That result is divided by the portfolio's Beta.

The formula tells you the portfolio's return over its market risk.

You can compare many portfolios this way, and we do. Which might have the highest ratio of return against risk?

After stress testing numerous portfolios for the Treynor Ratio and many other factors, I am convinced that there are certain managers that really "BEAT" the market. If a portfolio has a higher return than predicted by Beta, this often has to do with management skills.

Let us turn our attention to another measurement created by Michael Jensen, who looked at Alpha.

Alpha measures excess return over the Beta of a portfolio. Of course, a high Alpha might be achieved randomly or by luck, and that is why we look for managers that repeat good performance consistently, year after year. It is also why we never rely on any manager beating the market.

Beta is still the dominant factor we look at to create a portfolio logically. If Beta is 1.0, a portfolio with a Beta greater than 1.0 is as volatile as the market. On a risk-adjusted basis, sensitivity to the market goes as follows:

A beta of 1.0 means that for every 1% change in the market, an individual security or investment will likely move 1%. In other words, it tracks directly with the market. Stocks with betas greater than 1.0 have more amplified movements than the market itself; they have a greater level of risk. A beta, for example, of 1.4 implies that an investment's returns will likely be 1.4 times as volatile as that of the market. A beta of less than 1.0 means that the security moves in the same direction as the market, but not as far as the market. For example, a beta of .85 means that the security is 15% less volatile than the market.

We can also look at your behavioral finance profile to determine that.

As you know from prior Chapters, neither experienced management nor analytics alone rules the logic of investment decisions. When you scratch the surface, I am a value investor. I study financial data daily to look at the value of a company and what it means in a traditional business sense to invest in that company. What makes up a company's true value is not only what the market says a share is worth at the moment, but also the type of goods and services they offer - gross sales, net sales, the quality of management, cash flow, debt—all of this interests me.

I could think of no greater financial logician than Benjamin Graham, author of "The Theory of Investment Value" (Harvard University Press).

But, that book was written in 1938. Perhaps you have not heard of Graham, but you have heard of his student, Warren Buffet. There are many more mathematicians and economists who have studied whether there is a quantifiable relationship between value and portfolio performance. They did find that there is a positive relationship between your return and variables like price-earnings ratios, price-to-cash flow, price-to-book value. It just makes logical sense. If something has intrinsic value and is underpriced, the market will eventually find the true value, and you will make profits.

That is the lesson of my homey example about coffee, burgers and bagels where the stock price, but not the value of the food companies, plummeted because of remote circumstances in Greece.

I think it is fair for you to wonder why, with so many people studying the market, they cannot see what I see--that there are undervalued investments out there.

While I cannot guarantee that I have the answer, I am instinctively drawn to this conclusion. Most value investments are just not sexy. Value firms are usually in traditional businesses like food and transportation and not in digital health or technology. Depending on their size, they usually are not followed by many analysts and are little in the news--out of sight and out of mind to both you and even financial advisors and stock analysts.

For example, one of my favorite stocks is Lifeway Foods. I bet you never heard of it. Like many of my clients, I have been a stockholder over the past 20 years. They make Kefir, an Eastern European yogurt drink. Lifeway had 60 quarters of escalating revenues. Investors in this company had the ability to make up to two hundred and fifty times their money. But, this value company has gotten very little, if any, press.

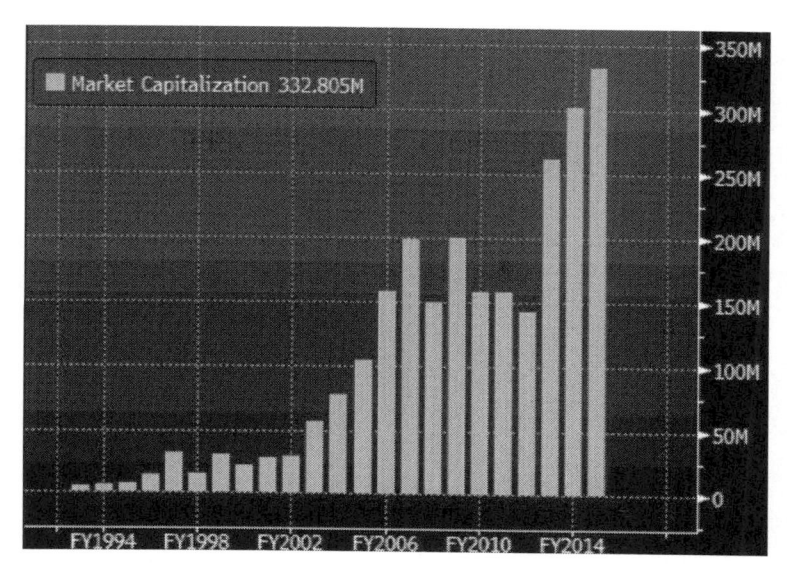

Lifeway--Market Capitalization Since 1994

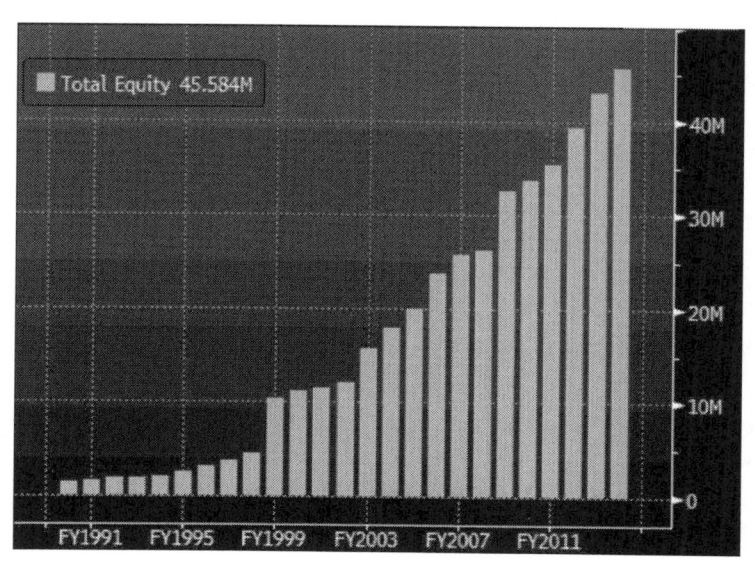

Lifeway--Total Equity Since 1991

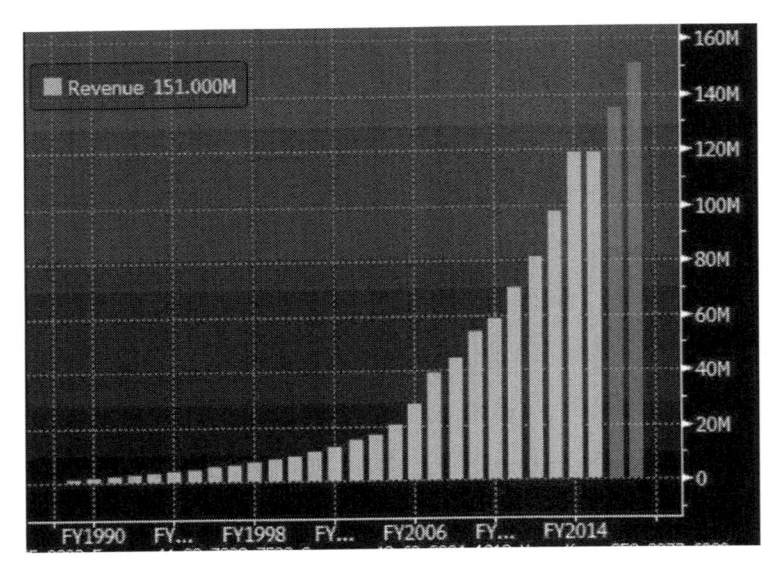

[Chart: Revenue 151.000M, bars from FY1990 to FY2014, scale 0 to 160M]

Whatever the reason that people by-pass value investments, I recommend that you focus logically, just as you would in any store. And now, I will give you another analogy that was shared by one of the women on our team. She mentioned that she had gone shopping at a fancy thrift shop and found a St. John's suit for $1,500, which was a nice bargain against $3,000 in the store bought new.

Two weeks later she patronized a different shop, in a different part of town that was not as fancy and upscale. She found the same St. John's suit for $23. How is this possible? She asked the thrift store manager how she had priced the suit. The thrift store manager answered, "The way I do all my suits - at $75 and then I drop the price as the weeks go by and no one buys." It was clear that the neighborhood women did not recognize the name St. John's as a valuable garment. The lesson here is simple: it does take know-how to get a spectacular bargain or an unprecedented investment return. But, they are out there.

How I Overlooked a Great Investment, Then Luckily Became Part of the Company

The stock, Stifel Financial, "SF," is one I deeply regret not learning about sooner. It's the best performing financial stock by a mile vs. its peers. I did not own a share of it and overlooked its brilliant management and persistently executed long-term strategy. As someone who makes frequent use the phrase "opinions die, but records stand," I completely missed the records. I was preoccupied with its bigger and more well-known competitors and their beautifully fluffed up commercials.

As of this writing, Stifle has returned a whopping 1,454% since 2003. By comparison, the next closest competitor was Raymond James with 267%. Goldman Sachs, assumed by many as the "smartest on the street," came in at 106%, followed by JP Morgan at 70%, and Morgan Stanley at 36%. Most of Stifle's other competitors actually managed to destroy shareholder value over the same period of time. We will not embarrass them here.

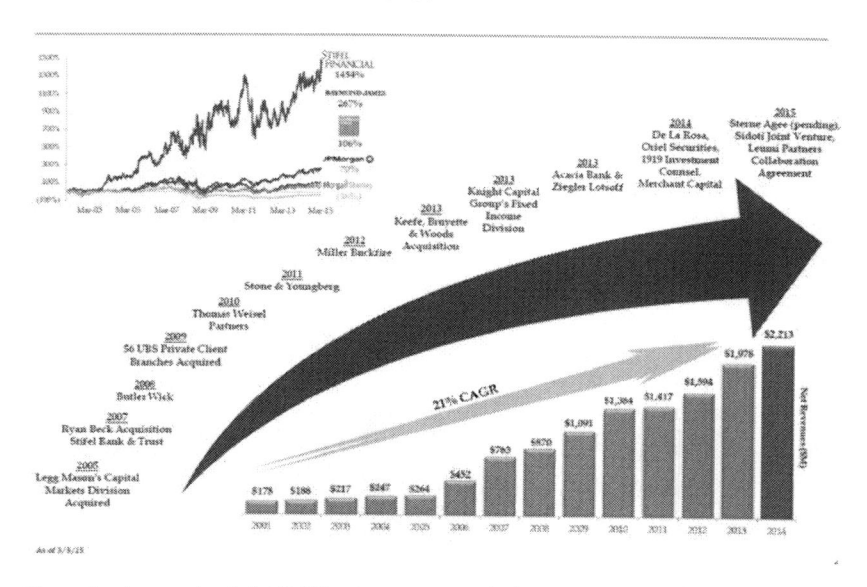

So what went right? First, as usual, it's the management. The company has been headed by its CEO, Mr. Ronald J.

Kruszewski. Conservatively run and not over-levered like many of its competitors, the company never had to take any of the TARP (Troubled Asset Relief Program), money offered to financial institutions during the financial crisis by the US Government to strengthen the weak. They were not involved in LIBOR or FX fixing, mortgage fraud, money laundering or tax evasion schemes, all of which were ramped and involved many of the top tier players. In fact, the fines and restitutions from that period totaled over $100 billion.

Ron made some incredibly lucrative and accretive acquisitions such as Thomas Weisel Partners, Keefe Bruyette & Woods, and Legg Mason's Capital Markets to name a few. They have compounded their core revenue by 22% and net income by 24% since 2006.

So let's get back to "opinions die, but records stand." Most companies, especially in the financial service industry, cannot sustain this type of success over such a long period of time unless they perform consistently for their clients. Happy clients will do more business. When they do more business, the company makes more in revenue. If you have a great management team, more revenue will translate into greater net income. When you have a greater net income, you grow your net worth. Those two factors make your company more valuable and your stock price performs appropriately. It goes up!! Is that logical enough?

In the summer of 2015, Ron decided to purchase the entire Barclay's US Wealth Management division, where I worked. He approached my team with an opportunity to work with him and use his infrastructure to implement my clients' plans. Believe me, when I tell you that most of his competitors were making my phone light up like a Christmas tree. They were telling me beautiful stories of performance, dedication, culture and success if I were to join them at their firm. All I could say is "opinions die, but records stand." Hopefully, if things go well, I can become one of the largest individual shareholders of the SF stock. Evidently, I am able to apply my logical analysis to career decisions as well.

Logical Asset Allocation:

In creating a logical asset allocation, you begin with a selection of asset classes that are truly different from each other in that they act differently under the same market conditions. Similarly, fund managers should have different qualities, some opportunistic others more conservative. In that way, an opportunistic manager will balance slow-growing, conservative assets with aggressive profits. Conservative investments will neutralize the occasional loss by the aggressive manager.

Then create a policy for your investing, a "business plan" for your future, where your life is the business entity. Watch the performance of your portfolio and keep the allocation in balance according to the original allocation policy. Make changes when your needs change, or you are suddenly exposed to more risk than you can currently handle, or you have met major goals and can become more opportunistic with excess capital.

Your investments policy should acknowledge your financial behavior, and your investment approach should be based on that financial behavior. Filter the rate of return that is your target, your needs, how you plan to make asset allocation decisions, which individual asset issues you will choose, the process you will employ to rebalance the allocation, and how often you plan to review your portfolio through the sieve of your financial behavioral temperament.

Finally, you must apply common sense to the individual investments you choose. Today in a low interest rate world, I constantly seek variable-rate bonds and income instruments. I am more tactically oriented. I do not rely on modern portfolio theory as the only strategy. I look at the past one- and two-year correlations of the assets classes as well as the past 20 years and take the average correlation of both. I think logically about what might be different today than in times past to affect performance of an asset.

And now the bottom line: Choose a system and stay true to it. The worst thing you can do is act rashly when the markets are inefficient and bail out. Actually, the markets go a little off once every 100 days. The second worst thing you can do is get nostalgic for 2008. Move on. That was then and this is now.

Never bet against the United States of America. It has 200 years of successfully solving its issues. We always come out on top. Don't bet against a 100% success rate.

As you will soon see, there is more to the logic of decision making to bring certainty into an increasingly uncertain world. In advanced planning, which we address in Part IV of this book, we focus on entrepreneurial concerns, your taxes, legacy and healthcare proxies. It is in this type of planning that you will gain more wealth than in any type of "investment deal" you will ever find.

Part IV: Entrepreneurs Need Bite

Chapter 19

Everyone Barks at the Entrepreneur

"The believer in the continued growth and prosperity of the United States, the progress of the largely undeveloped West, and the awakening South may safely assume a gradual and rapid growth in the value of railroad securities of these sections. The consensus of intelligent opinion points to the along continued improvement and advance."

The Pitfalls of Speculation, by Thomas Gibson, The Moody Corporation, 1906

I get along very well with entrepreneurs because I consider myself to be one. If you are an entrepreneur, we have a lot in common. If I have one piece of advice for you, it is, "Do not miss the forest for the trees."

The curse of the entrepreneur is that he or she is very busy.

Busy working on the business or in the business, it does not matter. The entrepreneur very rarely has time to work on investing. As you work hard and spend your 12 hour days in the office, do not lose sight of the forest for the trees. It is the end result of your business growth and capital investments that will allow you to enjoy the life you love, fulfill your hopes and dreams for your family, and if you wish, become a philanthropist.

Our team is very extensive and expanded. I am only one cog in the wheel of professionals that you will need for a successful business.

My readers who have already achieved success in more than one business know exactly what I am talking about. The lawyer, the accountant, the advanced tax professional, just to name a few, might be part of your team or ours. In any case, I know for sure I will be working closely with all of them.

Often, as team leader, I make sure that my investment decisions coordinate perfectly with the tax needs of the client. I am not a lawyer, but often one clause in a will or trust or an insurance rider will in some way be influenced by the investment I might suggest.

Once you have set up your advisory team, I hope, with our help, you will have the following people in place:

- Capital investors
- Insurance agent
- Corporate counsel (attorney)
- Personal attorney usually for trusts and estates
- Investment banker
- And, possibly, appraiser

Of course, this does not include your marketers, employees and partners.

For our purposes, part of The Bite is to get to know the people who surround you because mistakes are made for lack of coordination.

Perhaps you already have trusts and a will or gifting program created by your trusts and estates attorney. Perhaps these structures were created by other generations in your family and are perpetuated today.

But, if you are an entrepreneur, you need to think slightly differently. You might need additional strategic documents.

First, get the big picture. Ask yourself:

Am I planning to go public, sell the business, keep the proceeds and leave them in a trust or will?

With whom will I share these proceeds and when will they receive them?

How will I resolve any tensions in the family or competing interests between children and even children and a spouse?

The key is to chart out your family priorities.

From there, we can craft wealth management programs with structures to save hundreds of thousands in taxes and also maintain family harmony.

Programs and Strategic Documents for the Entrepreneur

Despite attention to the financial details of your life, I have discovered, in getting to know my entrepreneurial clients, that they can overlook certain documents and benefits that could be to their advantage. Without being exhaustive, here are a few I have found to be real problem solvers.

Grantor Retained Interest Trusts (GRAT)

Under a GRAT, beneficiaries are named and the circumstances under which they receive the principal and income are outlined. You receive income payments during your lifetime based on a formula.

Defective Grantor Trust (DGT)

With a DGT, you receive a promissory note for a business transfer and make periodic demands for its repayment.

Family Limited Partnership (FLP)

Under an FLP, you are the general partner. Income and assets devolve to the limited partners, perhaps children or grandchildren.

On our team, we often counsel that different types of stock be issued: restricted stocks, stock option plans, even when there are few employees.

We also ask clients to consider creating a family foundation dedicated to a cause that enhances the business but is quite separate from it.

Me with Former Governor David Paterson and Chris Cuomo

Chapter 20

The Four Problems of Successful Entrepreneurs

"The opinions of brokers are given a degree of credence to which they are seldom entitled, four, sad to relate, the lack of study and method is almost as prevalent behind me off is reeling as outside of it, in addition to which the desire to make commissions frequently leads the broker to an expression of encouraging views running parallel with the ideas of the client, whether such views are sincere or not. The empathetic opinions of friends and acquaintances are also greatly over-rated at times, especially if the advisor has been fortunate in his recent ventures, which fact alone is a dangerous and insufficient guide"

The Pitfalls of Speculation, by Thomas Gibson, The Moody Corporation, 1906

#1. Managing Debt Side

Here is an example of the biggest deal we have ever done. But, it works the same way with lower numbers.

A client owned a corporation earning several billion in revenue annually. He had a bank loan with the company as collateral paying 4% interest. He also had a private stock and bond portfolio worth $600 million.

I asked him if he ever thought of using his portfolio as security for a loan. He said "no," but the idea was very acceptable to him. In his case, money was lent at 1% against his securities. He paid down his loan of $300 million and saved an average of 3% in interest. After that move, we were saving $9,000,000 per year and the right to tap into his commercial bank loan at any time if needed.

In most cases, entrepreneurs are counseled not to mix their personal and business assets. That is because we generally foul things up when we do. But, when you have real expertise watching out for every detail, every minute, it can occasionally make sense. It did this time to the tune of $9,000,000 per year.

#2. Letting Things Slide

Busy. Busy, Busy. What is important in your life? What is important about the money that you have? What do you want to do at age 60?

We need to know ahead of time whether you are planning to retire in five years, or pass the business onto your children or stay on as a consultant. We even want to know these aspirations from very young entrepreneurs, even though we realize their big goals will change through the years.

#3. Not Getting Help Because You Think Your Business is Too Small

It is true our team's minimum under management per relationship usually ranges from $5,000,000-$10,000,000. But, we have also taken small accounts because we see breakthrough potential.

And, if you really do not fit with the type of help we offer, we can refer you to a boutique-size firm that specializes in small and growing companies. There are even strategic planners that specialize in particular industries. We use them for our clients all the time. Most importantly, we start with the exit strategy, the monetization or the succession planning. Do not be shy; get yourself help as early as you can.

#4. Succession Planning

90% of all Family Businesses Fail by the Third Generation. Will Yours?

Are you really ready to leave the business?

Are you totally confident that the relatives and employees you have groomed are ready?

Have you made plans for your next life stage?

Too infrequently do we consider the impact of aging on good, logical, rational decision making based on tax planning, legacy planning and wealth strategies. Over and over again, it is transparent to me that the client is procrastinating in transferring all or part of a family business. Excuses range from having the flu, to needing to travel, to even forgetting meetings.

What underlies this is the fear of losing one's identity and becoming invisible as we separate ourselves from a very fundamental part of our identity – that of business owner.

And while this is so easy for me to see in another, I am pretty sure I will be struggling with this myself.

It is hard to hand over the helm of a business you built or ran for most of your life if you think of succession planning as just a way to bow out gracefully. Consider, instead, that you are creating a blueprint of your values, mission and business wisdom for others to perpetuate for generations to come.

Of course, no one will ever completely play your role exactly as you do. But, you can create a strong Perpetuation Team by following four rules:

First, select a successor with your winning traits but also with additional skills for the new ways your company will need to do business in the future.

Second, when you select your protégée and the rest of the Perpetuation Team, do not be tempted to choose next of kin or siblings because you, or they, feel they are "entitled to be next in line."

Third, be fair but be strong. Do not put the wrong person in the wrong slot.

Fourth, do not hesitate to choose a team, not just one CEO or President. Things are more complex than when you started out and a variety of skills are needed.

With a team in place, it is time to create the infrastructure to perpetuate your business.

How will the business be governed? Who are your Executive, Legislature and Judiciary? In other terms, your CEO, Board and Conflict Resolver? You might want to make temporary appointments and see how your choices function while you are there to evaluate them.

A Code of Honor and Other Business Documents

Create a Code of Honor that perpetuates your ethical business practices, values, and includes the charitable causes you support.

Businesses that last through many generations always have a mission beyond material wealth and personal success to bind family members together for a higher purpose. You might want to produce a video featuring the people your charitable giving helps to inspire over the decades.

Only now are you ready to create the formal or legal documents that create the plan:

An arbitration or mediation clause resolves serious disputes.

Bylaws for a Family Advisory Council, for those not part of the Perpetuation Team, gives a forum for ancillary relatives with a financial stock for retired management to have input.

You probably already have a legal entity like a corporation, LLC or partnership. But, most family businesses fail because they overlook three structures that carry on their Charitable Mission and Code of Honor:

- **A Family Bank:** a funded trust which allows family members who work both in and outside the business to borrow and repay money for a stated purpose, like education or home buying. This avoids borrowing and debt among family members and the ensuing animosity so dangerous to a business.

- **A Family Mission Council:** a team to determine whether charitable aims are fulfilled. It is not necessary to create a Foundation or any complex legal structure. But, it is necessary to make the mission a centerpiece for running the business.

- **A Business Power of Attorney:** a document that appoints a team or individual to run the business if you are temporarily incapacitated. The appointment ends when you can take over again. The BPOA empowers your surrogate to continue charitable giving and restates the Code of Honor for conducting the business and making decisions.

Your business can easily disappear in less time than it took to build without a perpetuation plan. Do not let that happen to you.

The Loyalty Issue

Most successful entrepreneurs have an ad hoc team consisting of a lawyer and an accountant, maybe more than one. Sometimes adult children are on the team as well, or there is an in-house financial planner that only works for the family. Now, the entrepreneur begins to feel he or she needs more and would like to work with us.

All of a sudden there is a loyalty problem. People simply do not want to leave their "friends." Many of them started with advisors when they did not have much money, and these people helped them create the business and stayed with them. You have to learn to handle this loyalty issue.

The first thing we look at is how your advisor is being paid. If they are being paid on a percentage of how much is under management, then there is a conflict with our firm; and you will have to make a choice. If they are compensated for advice, we simply access them as a member of our team and work with them.

They are to be kept on and paid for their expertise. If a trusted advisor is useful for more than emotional reasons, we will work together. Yes, there may be some ruffled feathers at the beginning, but it does tend to work out.

On the other hand, if these people are controlling the assets, as they often are in a small family office, and really do not have the resources of accountants and attorneys your growing business now needs, we have to find out what they really bring to the table. If they have value, they continue to be properly compensated.

If their continued value is questionable, the entrepreneur has to make a tough personal decision between his family and his loyalty to a professional. I think you can guess who wins.

Financing as Part of Your Business Growth Process

I had a client with 30 medical offices. He spent a lifetime building his business. There was an economic benefit in having so many offices, not just from a revenue point of view, but for the price he could get by selling the chain rather than one at a time.

Because larger competitors had the ability to borrow at a low rate at that time, there were many companies seeking to acquire medical offices. He could sell his business, not work, and still get the same rate of return he was getting by working 24/7.

Like many entrepreneurs, he could not stand the thought of retirement. And in his mind that is all there was, run his business or do nothing. I showed him that by pricing it as a chain, he would receive 9- to 10-times its cash flow.

I brought in our investment bankers. They put a full structure together to show him how selling the entire business with financing for the buyer was a very good solution. But, we also worked with him so he could envision his future.

Let me explain one simple fact. This was not a touchy-feely process. We did not inspire him or tell him to go to a class on how to manage your time after retirement, or volunteer, or find his life purpose. Here is what we did.

I am a hard-core numbers guy and so was he.

We showed him the following:

Let us say his buyer wants to achieve a 15% rate of return on his investment. If his buyer finances the purchase of the chain at 7% versus 3% the buyer must make a lot more to reach the goal. By offering a buyer package with a low interest rate, we also could show any potential buyer how to pay much more for the business and still get 15%. That financing package is a huge benefit to everyone.

When our client saw how much he could get for his business, so much more than he thought, it did change his mind. He inspired himself with the freedom he would have to create his next life stage.

And now I have a little secret.

After all that paperwork and number crunching, the deal was actually not right for our investment banking firm. We sent it to another firm that did the deal for him. I think it is important that we never leave anyone in the lurch. Although we did not make much, it confirmed why we are here. And, the word spread.

If you are going to sell a business, it is logical to choose a period, like the present, when interest rates are low and the spread between the rates at which buyers can borrow over Treasury rates is slight. 'Cheap' borrowing creates a platform for asking a higher buying price.

And by the way, you can apply this 'sell when interest rates are low' strategy to a piece of real estate, as well.

Does your business need financing?

A client had a major stake in a private placement for the company that cleans and re-fluorinates fracking water. I liked the process so much that I personally invested. I thought it was a good idea.

Then the client came to me and said he would like to make some acquisitions for the company, and asked me to raise money for him. I went to the institutional client side of my firm, and we planned to raise $40-$50 million for the acquisitions.

After the acquisition process, revenue should have advanced from $30 to $75 million gross annually. This year it earned $24 million as the bottom line, after operating costs. Our next step would have been to help this company go public. As it turned out, we ultimately did not structure the deal; but did give the client the strategy he needed.

Insuring Your Business

I have an insurance license, but I really do not enjoy structuring insurance strategies. Nevertheless, it would be wrong of me not to explain that this is a big issue in everyone's life, particularly the entrepreneur. The fact is, you need insurance and probably lots of it. What you must study is competitive pricing.

Consider Key Man Insurance

Key Man insurance is an important form of business insurance. There is no legal definition for "key person insurance." In general, it can be described as an insurance policy taken out by a business to compensate that business for financial losses that would arise from the death or extended incapacity of an important member of the business.

Key man insurance is a standard life insurance policy that is used for business succession or business protection purposes.

The policy's term does not extend beyond the period of the key person's usefulness to the business. Key man insurance policies are usually owned by the business, and the aim is to compensate the business for losses incurred with the loss of a key income generator and facilitate business continuity. Key person insurance does not indemnify the actual losses incurred but compensates with a fixed monetary sum as specified in the insurance policy.

Many businesses have a key person, such as the owner, who is responsible for the majority of profits or is unique and hard to replace. The business may take out a key person insurance policy on the life or health of any employee whose knowledge, work or overall contribution is considered uniquely valuable to the company.

The business does this to offset the costs (such as hiring temporary help or recruiting a successor) and losses (such as a decreased ability to transact business until successors are trained) which the employer is likely to suffer in the event of the loss of a key person.

Most people do not make the connection between death benefit insurance, succession planning and family feelings. But, boy, the connection is huge.

Entrepreneurs worry about strife in the family. If there is a sale of the business, how will the money be split between those that have worked in the business and those that have not?

If there is succession planning, what should you do for the person, usually a child, who is not working in the business? Often, making the person who has not gotten the business interest the beneficiary of a death benefit insurance policy, which accumulates cash value through the years, is better than all the smooth feelings and heartfelt discussions you can have.

We try to plan so that friction does not take place. Part of it is making sure everyone knows what to expect. Another part is funding the succession properly. We start with a set of questions, not only about what our client wants, but what their heirs and beneficiaries want as well.

With a good handle on expectations, you, as the matriarch or patriarch, must take leadership. Do you see your whole family as part of a succession plan or just some of your children or other loved ones? When there is a second marriage with older children and very young children, there often are hard feelings on many sides.

Goals and values must be reconciled. It is my deep concern, and perhaps yours too, that with all the personal issues on our plate, we might simply let things slide. My role is to look at the economic barriers and help you overcome them.

Some of the biggest challenges that I have identified include:

- Business valuation data
- Loss of brand when the founder leaves
- Training of takeover personnel and leadership
- Decisions with regard to governance
- Long-term positioning, compensation and family plan

Fortunately, there are sophisticated approaches including stock ownership plans, family limited partnerships and various trusts that can save the day and unravel the mystery.

As dicey as transferring your business can be, restructuring your life after selling or transferring the business leads you into greater unchartered territory.

Entrepreneurs, or anyone else for that matter, rarely think of relying on a wealth advisor to help them sort out their next life stage. But, your wealth manager may know more about you, your hopes, dreams and goals, and what has caused you misery than almost anyone else. I like to say that I have the 30,000-foot view, not only of my client's portfolios but of who my clients are.

Way before a sale or IPO or grappling with any transfer issues, part of what I consider The Bite is to start "after planning." Are you interested in philanthropy? Personally, I am. When I was asked to include one picture for this book, I was excited about a picture of myself with some wonderful kids. I hope that my work and my funding supported their life.

Most of my clients are charity minded, have causes and have tucked away things that they would like to do when they get a chance. The time to pull out these fulfilling life wishes is not after you have made your sale or transfer, but before.

You would be surprised how understanding your wealth will help you in all of your life goals. You might create a family foundation that gives purpose to the lives of younger family members that seem to be going astray. Would an individual that you love who is not appropriate to be in the family business do great in the business of philanthropy?

Will you take the future by the horns and find a new and greater purpose than ever before? And, can you do all of this in the context of saving taxes, preserving income and creating trusts that benefit you and your cause?

It may seem strange to you that this Chapter is a Chapter of questions rather than answers.

There are answers and solutions to every question and every issue in the days after your business transition. The trick is not to find the right answer. We can do that for you. Your task is to ask the right questions and ask them early.

You cannot imagine the relief and reduction of anxiety when you have a vision for your life, including your wealth management, after you have divested yourself of your business obligations. Notice that I never use the word retirement. My clients do not plan for retirement. They do plan for next stages in their life, which are usually more exciting than they had ever anticipated.

Whether you form a charitable remainder trust or you plan to fund a nongovernmental organization (NGO), we can help. The team is there. We have The Bite. I encourage you to come in and have a candid discussion with our team. We will discuss how you see your future. The purpose is to give you greater clarity.

Warning: Stormy Weather Ahead

In our discussion of these lofty goals we inevitably also uncover problems. They might be issues from a first marriage, ownership of offshore property, temporary cash flow issues because of how a sale was structured.

If you have a buyer for your business in mind, we must be sure of the credit-worthiness of that buyer and evaluation figures. Often your life plans for the future will not work out if the buyout has not been structured to meet your needs. What might seem to be a private lifestyle decision actually impacts your financial decisions and vice versa.

In my introduction to this book, I talked about behavioral psychology and investing. We explored why we buy high and sell low instead of the other way around. If fear of loss comes into the picture, this is doubly so as we age.

When we have divested ourselves of our business, we have sold our "cash cow." We became wealthy because of our business. Now what? Many of the wealthiest entrepreneurial clients came to me as an advisor only after they sold their business. For decades before, they did not consult because, in their minds, the great bulk of their money needed to be reinvested in their business.

Oddly enough, the first time they ever met with any full-scale wealth advisor was after the sale of their business.

They usually retain the same risk-tolerant money personality they had when they were 20. Only now they are 60, 70, 80 years of age.

Most of my entrepreneurial clients were the bosses. People came to them for advice, not the other way around. They were and are quick decision makers, confident and smart.

I have said many times that I pride myself in having some of the smartest clients in the universe. But, what they know is their business, not wealth management. And, it can be hard for anyone with an independent, entrepreneurial spirit to let someone else take over even when they are swimming in totally new waters.

This is a time of great vulnerability, where they are more likely than not to fall for The Bark and be blinded by The Fluff. Some of the smartest people on earth are the ones who were conned by Bernie Madoff.

Those are extreme cases. More often entrepreneurs are likely to hook up with a mediocre, well-meaning, honest advisor; but one that really does not have the total picture or that 30,000-foot view. When we meet, we look at a lot more than your bottom line. We look at your cash flow and your buying power.

Another post sale or transfer issue for many entrepreneurs is maintaining the value of the cash they took out of the business. This means consideration of world currencies and an asset mix that takes inflation into account even when inflation is low at the moment.

After all, your income will no longer change by your increasing prices or decrease the cost of manufacture. You are not in the business anymore. It is your personal assets that must do the work which commerce once did for you.

A word about burnout:

I have found that my entrepreneurial clients work so hard and have worked so many hours a day for so many years that they do not even realize they are burning out. They may be on automatic pilot until their business is successfully sold or transferred. But, then, a crash.

With encouragement and understanding, they will take a rest. Sometimes that rest lasts only a weekend, sometimes a couple of years. They return as refreshed, energetic and ready to embrace life as they did in what is sometimes erroneously called their 'peak years' of the 40s and 50s.

If they have created a wealth management system that supports them and those dependent on them while they take their life's breather, there is no telling what they can create in the decades ahead. We all know of successful entrepreneurs that became artists, writers, philanthropists or started other businesses, perhaps in highly unrelated fields, that grew bigger and more successful than their first.

Sometimes, it is hard to admit that you need a rest. But imagine how freeing it is to work with a team that understands that your rest is really for rejuvenation. This is not the end of anything, but a hiatus between successes. The way we will structure your portfolio and manage your wealth takes a very different turn because we understand that most entrepreneurs are very much like the unsinkable Molly Brown. Wealth protection is the lifeboat that will carry them, and they will emerge to succeed another day.

Chapter 21

Before the Parade Passes By

"The idea that large properties cannot be investigated intelligently is a mistake. Every standard listed security must, under the rules of a well conducted exchange, offer to the public every facility for such investigation.... The man who speculates in a business-like manner will lead one see the necessity of entirely eliminating abnormal possibilities and rashness from his plan of operation. The difference between expecting from the market what is reasonable and expecting too much; and between buying what can be reasonably protected, and even increased, and plunging, is exactly the difference between success and failure."

The Pitfalls of Speculation, by Thomas Gibson, The Moody Corporation, 1906

Sometimes, it is just the right time to sell. Not seeing that could cost you a fortune. Our first job is to help you determine whether the right time to sell is coming up. It may be so because of your life needs, because of the market or because of completly disruptive shifts.

Or, as we outlined in a past Chapter, because interest rates are low and buyers who finance can pay more for your business.

Sometimes it is our duty to suggest a sale, although you are always the decision maker. Other times, it is just the right tax time.

That is why our evaluation team may be one of the most important groups to the entrepreneur. And, we will structure the sale very much dependent on the reason why a sale is important to you.

- Is there an illness?
- Is the business underperforming?

- Is there a paradigm shift that might make the business less desirable in the next five years?
- Is there a new passion that has taken over?
- Is money needed to start a new and more lucrative business?

The Man I Met on the Train

I was having a private discussion on my cell phone with one of my Russian clients while riding on a train. We were speaking in English. I sensed that someone was listening in. I switched to Russian. The eavesdropper and I were sitting on a two-seater bench. I spoke for only a few minutes.

When I hung up the guy next to me, whom I certainly did not know, was Russian, turned to me and said, "So how did that go?" Well, we hit it off right away, and we started doing business from then on. Believe it or not, that was a $20 million account. Yep, I am a lucky guy.

But, I was genuinely fascinated by his business. He owned a logistics company that made same-day deliveries of packages. They deliver everything, including healthcare-related materials, to hospitals. It grew dramatically, as you might imagine, and has one of the best profit margins in this sector, with hundreds of trucks and drivers everywhere.

This gentleman is 60 years old and has an adult son. What was really on his mind was the transfer of his wealth and the business. What he needed was an investment banker who would structure a sale of his business or create a succession plan which would carry on the business for multiple generations.

Other alternatives to a sale that might serve you better, such as creating a stock employee ownership company, bringing on a partner, transferring assets to family, are all considered in the mix.

Often the most important question for the entrepreneur is whether he or she will sell for cash or keep an interest in the business.

We ask one question. If you plan to keep an interest, what's your motivation?

With integrated pre-sale planning, we gain clarity and develop a plan that is all part and parcel of your wealth management overview.

My Wealth Management Philosophy

I have worked with many fine firms throughout my career. I am always aware that you are paying me for my services. A wealth manager has a tremendous amount of legal and compliance responsibilities. All of these were set out by the legislature or the courts to protect clients because there are so many opportunities to hurt individuals, even through honest advice.

But, I think we must go farther than what the law requires in our management due diligence philosophy. Ever since I became a wealth manager, I have had my own take on right and wrong. A wealth manager's Code of Honor, if you will.

Compensation should be based on performance.

That means compensation is based on a percentage of the amount under management. If our performance is less, our compensation is less. As your portfolio grows, our compensation grows. We are in a financial partnership with our client's portfolios.

Part V

Financial Life Management

Chapter 22

The Art of Advanced Planning

The concept of advanced planning reflects an acknowledgment that wealth management through investing is only a small part of what you should expect of a financial advisor.

Traditional advanced planning focuses on financial strategies to protect your wealth. But, at The Moldaver Group, it also emphasizes life strategies such as where you plan to live after retirement, or how you plan to send your children to college, which has now easily become a quarter of million dollar tariff.

Advanced planning also encompasses tax planning, legacy planning, business succession, planning for multi-generations, planning for longevity and lifelong independence.

It is a complicated world, and advanced planning might also include planning for blended families, deciding to have children later in life, going from a two-paycheck to a one-paycheck family, taking a sabbatical or turning your hobby into a business.

Advanced planning might also be seen from the point of view of an older generation for which planning includes never being a burden to your family, even if you have a chronic care need. Advanced planning can be seen from the point of view of an adult child, who is a caregiver to that older parent and must balance their own work life with their caregiving responsibilities.

Today, many boomers are de facto fiduciaries for older parents with responsibilities to siblings who may live farther away from parents. These responsibilities can cause a conflict between parents' needs, their desire to leave a legacy, and accountability to siblings who are out of touch with the day-to-day expenditures that the age of longevity now demands.

Advanced planning requires that we think ahead. Like a chess game, "three deep."

The Fluff of the Certifications

There is an FINRA website that has pages and pages of various impressive titles that investment professionals can have if they take courses.
www.finra.org/investors/professional-designations

Take a look at the prerequisites. Most do not measure up to having a finance degree, certainly not a law degree specializing in trust and estates. Many of these titles sound impressive, but there is a huge difference among them.

I recall a brochure offering the title of Retirement Specialist and all you had to do to qualify was to read a three-hour online module and answer a bunch of questions at the end. Really?

My point is not to bash any additional education, I think it is wonderful. I am simply saying if you want the best, then use the gold standard. Use a CFA- Certified Financial Analyst, use the top trust and estates attorney. As with everything that we discuss in this book, there is The Fluff, The Bark, and The Bite of designations.

For example, not only do I want an attorney to work with me; but I want a great one with years of experience. I want that lawyer sitting next to me and available ALL the time. That's why I always work with a boutique type of firm or a large firm that gives me a boutique environment in which I can do the best for my clients.

When it comes to making investment judgments, that is my specialty.

For the rest, I work on spotting problems as well as solving them. That is a big job in itself. If you miss a red flag in the taxable estate planning of a client, for example, you would never realize they need a tax specialist.

True, some advisors are familiar with a few solutions, like a family trust, spousal trust, a generation-skipping trust, probate avoidance, and have a few formulas that can help. But, that does not make them an expert.

Nor does TheFluff of certifications take the place of a law or CPA education and experience. Thinking so can be dangerous Bark, as you might not see a specialist because you believe your advisor has deep enough knowledge.

This is often far from the case. Expertise is particularly important for the entrepreneur and other clients that have complex needs.

Ultra high net worth folks need experts that know their bailiwick on a granular level. The Fluff of certifications does not replace the need for experts that keep up with and concentrate on a single area of expertise. My job is to get you the right expert.

Then there is the special skill of getting your experts to talk with each other so the analyst and the estate planner know what each other is thinking.

And here is an aspect of moneymaking which I do not consider Fluff - that is knowing all about my clients. I need to know on a very basic level if you have a heart condition, are planning a trip around the world, getting a divorce and remarrying. This impacts how all the experts will make professional decisions and help you make personal decisions.

Just because I see my mandate as making you good returns consistently, does not mean that I do not take into account each and every personal trait and circumstance which may impact your financial future.

In my first book, you will read a set of questions that we ask all of our clients which I have put in Appendix I here.

The questions are for the purpose of helping us identify red flags and possible issues in the future, as well as to understand what is going on with you right now. All of our team will have your answers to those questions, and I will know everything about you by the time we finish with the initial interview.

We update this information as our relationship continues. At our initial meeting, we may already have other group members present. In any case, they all know everything and understand who you are.

Make sure, when you select advisors, that even if they have deep expertise in their own field, they are not working in a silo. Make sure there is one person who is overlooking all five aspects and can bring everyone together. In my case, that 'overseer' is me. I oversee everything, so I know everything, not only about the client, but about the thinking of the specialists with whom I am working.

Consider the "Death Put."

Here is an example of advanced planning that might not come to mind until there is a crisis unless you are working with an advisor. That is the use of what is called "the death put." A risk-reducing strategy to use with long-term bonds, so that if the holder passes away prior to maturity, his or her heirs can cash in the bond at its full maturity value.

Many older adults are interested in protected income. Right now we are in a low interest rate market, but your best deals are with long-term bonds. Nevertheless, bonds fluctuate in value, and you take market risk and may lose principle if you sell before the maturity date.

That is a dilemma for many older adults. They would like to buy long-term bonds at the higher rate but may not realistically live long enough to cash in at the full maturity value.

They could assure that their loved ones would get the full par value of the bond even if they passed away prior to maturity, and they would enjoy the extra cash flow from a long-term bond during their lifetime by using a death put. This is just one way that, within your parameters of risk tolerance, you can simply get better results with advanced planning/thinking!

It is not a misnomer to consider advanced planning an art rather than a science.

While we can stress test a portfolio for its efficiency and arrive at a quantifiable analysis, no computer can help us determine what's best for your parents, or how to distribute gifts among your children. That planning needs your intense participation and our caring approach to your personal needs.

Nevertheless, there are some factors in advanced planning that are common to all of our clients and strategies that are unique to the way The Moldaver Group approaches the art of advanced planning creatively.

Chapter 23

A Word about Tax Planning

"After a careful examination, covering a period of ten years, and a study of the methods of successful and unsuccessful traders as shown in some thousands of speculative accounts, the following facts are adduced:

1st-The greatest causes of loss in speculation are ignorance, over speculation, and carelessness, of importance in the order named."

The Pitfalls of Speculation, by Thomas Gibson, The Moody Corporation, 1906

In the next 5 years, over 1 trillion dollars in assets will be inherited, much of it by Uncle Sam. Would it surprise you to learn that in 1998, two Philadelphia Inquirer reporters, Bartlett and Steele, won the Pulitzer Prize for uncovering 600 private inheritance tax exemptions voted into the 1986 Internal Revenue Code by various congressmen?

One such exemption applied only to persons from Texas who died at age 75 on Oct. 28, 1983, residing in Tarrant County and with estates of under 12.5 million.

At the time I write this. no one is clear as to the fate and the extent of the estate tax in the future. In fact, we are not sure what will happen to income taxes, capital gains or gift tax. In the face of this uncertainty, we more than ever work with your tax professionals on an ongoing basis.

Throughout this part of the book, you will discover all types of strategies we have used to save taxes in a legitimate time-honored manner. But, none of them may hold in the future. My point is that advanced planners must keep in constant touch with the tax consequences of each transaction.

Nevertheless, let us address a few of the biggest tax pitfalls we have encountered for the type of client we usually serve, one with a high net worth and a tax gun to their head.

Avoid the Three Biggest Estate Planning Mistakes

1. Believing that the proceeds of a life insurance policy are inherited tax-free. Insurance is counted in your gross estate if you die owning the policy, are able to change beneficiaries, take loans against it or can dictate how dividends are applied.

2. Giving gifts with strings attached, keeping access to the money or having tacit agreements to give it back. Such "conditional gifts" are still your money according to the IRS.

3. Thinking that a revocable, so-called "living trust," or "probate avoiding trust" saves taxes. It doesn't!

Important Things to do to Save Taxes

We work with many attorneys, and they have taught me a thing or two. Here are a few strategies that have saved our clients a great deal in taxes through the years. Some are less important under current tax laws, but we have a feeling that taxes will creep up again. So, we stay current.

- **If you are married,** put a clause in your will or probate-avoiding trust allowing the trustee or executor to allocate up to the maximum Federal Exclusion to the trust, and name your spouse the beneficiary of income and your kids the beneficiary of the principal when your spouse dies.

- **Anyone** can set up a charitable remainder trust. You will get an income tax deduction, increase your income stream, and get tax-free money to your heirs by buying a replacement insurance policy in the amount of the charitable gift.

- **If you own a family business** and plan to transfer it to children, sell your common stock over time to the kids in return for a private annuity. IRS tables set up the amount of the annuity depending on age, value of business and more.

- **If you have a lot of investment in real estate,** it will be subject to probate in both the state in which it is located and perhaps in your state of residence, as well. Hint--transfer real estate to a corporation and own shares in the corporation instead of owning the real estate outright. Then the probate will take place only in the state where you resided at time of death.

While taxes used to be a central focus in advanced planning, lately healthcare has taken center stage. Let us look at how you have planned for healthcare in the next Chapter.

Me and Wayne Chrebet in the Office

Chapter 24

To Your Health

An average couple can expect to spend $225,000 in healthcare in their lifetime, out of pocket. You might wonder how this is possible given insurance policies and Medicare.

First, the healthcare I speak of is long-term care, covered by Medicare only after a hospital stay and only for skilled care, and then only for a limited period of days.

Second, long-term care can be needed at any age. In fact, 40% of Americans needing long-term care today are working age adults ages 18-64. Only about 10% of nursing home patients are under 65, so most of these younger people needing long-term care are being cared for in the community, at a very large sacrifice from their family members.

How Will You Cover Long-Term Care Costs?

Pros and Cons of Self-Insuring

I have been forthcoming that most of my clients are wealthy. They could afford to self-insure and spend money from assets in case they do have long-term care needs. Most could renovate their home and pay for a nurse or attendant at home. But, many prefer insurance, particularly well-chosen long-term care insurance.

This is an insurance product that fell out of favor as rates rose on unsuspecting purchasers. But, today these rate increases are regulated. Still, you need to know the pros and cons of buying a policy, which is not inexpensive, if you buy in your late 50s or early 60s. Even at age 80, you are eligible, but prices rise as the risk taken on by the issuance company increases for older applicants.

There are six choices that impact your premium. Here is each choice and a recommendation guideline.

- Daily or Monthly Benefit- Look at the average cost in your area and buy a daily or monthly benefit as high as you can afford- even $150 more than the average cost in your area if you can afford it. Inflation is strong, and you'll probably need the extra benefit at claim time.

- Waiting Period (Elimination Period) - Most people will choose a waiting period (deductible) of 100 days or less. If you have over $1 million in assets (not counting your house and car), you can look at waiting periods of greater than 100 days. If you have assets less than $1,000,000, definitely choose a shorter waiting period like 60, 30, or 20 days. Look at policies that require only one waiting period in a lifetime.

- Benefit Period/Benefit Maximum - Choose at least three years or longer if you can afford it.

- Inflation Protection - This benefit is a must if you are age 70 or under. Choose the method that makes your benefits grow 5% compounded every year for the rest of your life.

- Home Health and Community Coverage - If you have someone to live with who can be a primary caregiver, you can select coverage that will pay them (if it is an option on the policy you are considering). If you are young (30's-50's) and you do not know if you will have a primary family caregiver in the future, take the option if you can afford it, so you will have maximum choice at claim time.

Tips for Benefit Choices in Group Plans

Inflation Coverage- If you are offered the opportunity to buy a plan that guarantees that your daily or monthly benefit will grow automatically each year as long as you hold the policy, take it. The premium will be more, but your benefit has a much better chance of keeping up with the rising cost of long-term care. Also, if you have a claim, your benefit will continue to grow and, in most plans, your premium will stop. The automatic increases should grow compounded (not simple) each year and only the benefit should increase annually, not the premium.

Home Health Care - Many group plans offer benefits that cover long-term care outside of the nursing home, such as home health care, adult day care, etc. as an option. You are well advised to take it. It is expected that since nursing home beds are over 87% occupied today, and is very expensive, more and more ways to provide future long-term care in the community is the trend. And, most people would rather be cared for at home as long as possible, anyway.

Non-forfeiture/Return of Premiums Benefits - Many group plans offer an option that allows you (or your beneficiary) to get your premiums back or keep some of the benefits if you cancel your policy or die without using it. Extra premium is charged for this privilege, so analyze carefully if the extra premium is a wise expenditure. You might be better off putting the extra premium in your 401K or other retirement fund or use it to buy a higher level of benefit: an increased dollar amount of coverage, or better inflation or home care benefits.

Should You Self-Insure?

Let us say a premium is $2,200 a year. In ten years earning 10%, a $2,,200 a year investment equals $38,500, enough to pay for only one year of a nursing home in the lowest cost areas. The average stay in a nursing home is 19 months, according to the Brooking Institute, but home care is much longer. Alzheimer's patients live 8-20 years with the disease, and that is rising. And are you getting 10% guaranteed on your investments? You be the judge whether you can self-insure, based on your family history of both health and successful money management.

What about Medicaid and Medicare? Won't They Pay?

Medicaid is a poverty program for the blind, disabled and those over 65 with low assets and income. For the most part, my readers will not be eligible. You may have heard that you can transfer assets to a trust or gift assets outright to qualify. But, trusts must be established five years or more before applying for Medicaid; and you cannot exercise any control or receive an income stream.

Although our clients do not qualify for Medicaid, we believe that keeping up with the program and maintaining relationships with Elder Law attorneys is part of advanced planning, because our reach is multigenerational. Often the parents of our clients face the danger of dissipation of assets when care is needed.

Of greatest importance in our brand of advanced planning is the use of the Power of Attorney (POA).

The POA is, pound for pound, the single most important health planning and estate planning tool available to you.

There are three types that take effect at different times and under different circumstances:

- Traditional - the traditional POA designates someone you trust to act on your behalf as long as you are around and capable. It is used by people who want to temporarily give someone else control of their finances. For example, a POA designating a spouse to close on a piece of property while you are away on a business trip, or an arrangement with a money manager to make trades in your brokerage account at their discretion until you revoke the power.

- Durable - this POA is the most often used. It continues even if you are mentally or physically incompetent. Its purpose is to allow loved ones to handle your money on your behalf, to make a gift, to fund a trust, do estate planning and pay your insurance premiums so policies do not lapse. It is essential for every one of us.

- Springing power - this "springs to use" only after a person becomes incompetent. It takes the written confirmation of the treating physician to confirm mental or physical incompetency. It has the same purpose as the durable power but is suitable for those with less close and trusted relatives and for those who do not want the power to be effective while they can act on their own behalf.

All three types of powers can be either general or limited.

A general power gives control over all financial tasks. A limited power specifies tasks, like check writing, stock trading, rent collection, etc.

POA Checklist

Make sure that your POA form contains the following:

- Whether multiple attorneys-in-fact must act together or whether one can act separately for all.

- A clear method for choosing a successor attorney-in-fact.

- A clear specification of powers that are included and/or excluded.

- Durability language: "This Power of Attorney shall not be affected by the subsequent disability or incompetence of the principal. This is intended to be a Durable Power of Attorney."

- Statement that the power is valid and may be relied upon by a third party.

- Every power must be signed, witnessed and notarized by both you and the attorney-in-fact.

Living Will - How to Stay in Control of Your End of Life Medical Care

A living will is neither a will nor anything involved with living - that is just a euphemism to make the idea more palatable. It is really a declaration of the level of life support devices you want to be used in the case of a terminal illness. In most cases, the patient cannot respond coherently or at all when the time comes. Their written wishes take the place of their present expression.

So, what do you want for yourself? No one ever promised you an easy question. All I can do is to show you how to keep control of your medical care.

Three Choices for Living Wills

- **The Health Care Proxy** - you delegate the decision to another person - essential for those in non-traditional relationships; not good if you have no close loved one.
- **The Living Will** - if you DO NOT want the plug pulled away, say so; most forms favor termination of support.
- **The Health Care Power of Attorney** - same as the proxy except you can add specific wishes and give powers if circumstances are different than foreseen.

Dangerous Healthcare Documents and How to Fix Them

As you can see, the Power of Attorney and the healthcare proxy can and should give instructions on how you want your healthcare and your money arranged when you can no longer make a decision.

But, there are pitfalls.

Here is an outstanding article written by Adriane Berg, CEO of Generation Bold, a business development company to reach boomers, caregivers and the mature. She coined the phrase "Longevity Law," used by many attorneys today.

Longevity Document Dangers

And How to Fix Them

By Adriane Berg

The fastest growing demography in America are those over the age of 85. While most of us age well, we all need specialized legal documents that assure us lifelong control over our money and our healthcare during mental or physical incapacity.

These documents are: Powers of Attorney that appoint surrogates to carry out your financial wishes, and Health Care Powers of Attorney or Health Care Proxies that appoint a surrogate to carry out your health care wishes. Living Wills and Do Not Resuscitate Orders are also used in many states to express your wishes regarding extraordinary measures like life support.

Without these documents, there is danger that the court will appoint a conservator or guardian to take over your money and health care decisions, at considerable cost and often heart break for you and your family. Or that doctors, institutions or the legislature will impose their decisions at critical times.

But, these crucial documents can also be a danger to our health or wealth, if they do not adequately and clearly express your desires.

Here are the pitfalls and how to avoid them.

#1. Danger - The document is ineffective just when you need it.

A Power of Attorney is a document that appoints an agent to act as your substitute. It authorizes your agent to access and spend your money, to buy, sell or gift your investments, your personal and real property, to sign your name to other documents, cash checks, file your taxes, and do a host of other financially related activities.

Most people sign these powers of attorney for use if they become incapacitated and cannot act for themselves. But a traditional Power of Attorney is extinguished if you become incapacitated. It strips your surrogate of the power to act, just when you need a substitute to act for you.

The Fix:

Create a "Durable" Power of Attorney, which is effective (unless specifically revoked by you) no matter what your mental or physical condition. Durable powers take effect immediately upon signing, and continue in force whether or not you have capacity. The document must specifically state that it is durable and remains in effect upon your incapacity.

#2. Danger - The Document Gives Control To Others Too Soon

Since a Power of Attorney (durable or standard) takes effect immediately upon signing, you are giving over power while you're still able to handle your own affairs, and make your own decisions.

The Fix:

The "Springing" Power of Attorney "springs" to life when two physicians certify that you have incapacity, whether temporary or permanent, that prevents you from handling your affairs. Your surrogate can act for you only if and when you are incapacitated, and, you take back the helm on regaining capacity.

Idea for Entrepreneurs: Create a separate "Springing" Business Power of Attorney. While most powers of attorney carefully spell out when they take effect, rarely do they spell out how to regain control. A well thought-out Business Power of Attorney can be flexible enough to allow you to keep control over your business for as long as possible even as competency waxes and wanes.

#3. Danger - The Directions are Incomplete or Just Plain Wrong

Many Powers are "one size fits" all computer generated forms that do not take account of your needs or wishes.

The Fix:

The Power should make sure your medical bills are paid, your insurance premiums are met, your mortgage is satisfied, your taxes are paid and your affairs are managed. Powers can be "general," affording the power to the surrogate to do anything you can legally do, or "limited," specifying one or several distinct activities. Significant to our longevity, both the Durable and Springing Power can establish your wishes regarding spending money for home health care.

For example:

It is understood that it is my overriding wish to stay in my home in the event of incapacity; therefore I authorize my agent to make expenditures for home renovations, at home medical equipment, medication management, mobility devices, motion sensors and the services of a geriatric care manager and any other expenditures to create a state of the art environment.

Idea for Long-Term Care: Give your agent sufficient power to plan for government benefits that cover long-term health care costs. Strategies include gifting assets or placing them in trust. Since most people name their closest heirs as their surrogate, there may be a conflict of interest, so consider a separate Gifting Power of Attorney, naming as surrogate, a person who will not also be the recipient of the gift.

#4. Danger - The Health Care Directive is Too Vague

Without clear health care directives, decisions regarding your medical care, custodial care and even your end of life planning will be out of your hands. The quality of your final years, days and moments may have very little resemblance to what you would have wanted.

The Fix:

Say it like you want it.

Long-Term Care: Set out your preferences regarding your care during a long-term or chronic illness.

Coordinate your directives with your Durable or Springing Power of Attorney.

Make sure that the agent handling your money, and arranging for the payment of your desired care is not in conflict with your health care agent. One easy fix is to make them the same person. If you have the clause in your Power of Attorney for "aging in place" in your home, make sure that a similar clause exists in your health care power.

Pain Treatment: A typical clause gives your surrogate the power:

To consent to and arrange for the administration of pain-relieving drugs of any kind or other surgical or medical procedures calculated to relieve my pain, including unconventional pain-relief therapies that my Agent believes may be helpful to me, even though such drugs or procedures may lead to permanent physical damage, addiction, or even hasten the moment of (but not intentionally cause) my death.

Idea for Family Surrogates: Whether you opt for discontinuing life support in the event that physicians feel there is no hope, or for aggressive treatment, such as continued "machine assistance", "heroic surgeries" or repeated defibrillations, make sure that your agent, (usually a child or your spouse) understands your desires, and is on your wavelength. The American Bar Association, www.americanbar.org, and the National Academy of Elder Law Attorneys, www.naela.com, have helpful material on holding a conversation with the family on End of Life Preferences.

#6-Danger-Your Surrogate Will Re-Interpret or Ignore Your Wishes

There are legal and criminal sanctions for surrogates who ignore your wishes deliberately, or self deal with your money. But, the more frequent problem is the honest fiduciary, including a professional trustee, concerned with liability to your heirs if they spend large sums on your health care.

The Fix:

One way to handle this is to specifically relieve your trustee or other surrogate, of liability to your heirs if they spend too freely on your health care, so long as the decisions are in accordance with your expressed wishes. Such a clause may look like this:

My Trustee and my Trustee's estate, heirs, successors, and assigns are hereby released and forever discharged by me, my estate, my heirs, successors, and assigns from all liability and from all claims or demands of all kinds arising out of the acts, except for willful misconduct or gross negligence, needed to carry out my wishes as expressed in clause (specify the relevant clause in your trust) of this Trust.

And so, the key to advanced planning in the age of longevity is consistency and communication.

For the affluent client, there is great danger of poor execution of wishes. Quality of life expenditures, like home companions and life style maintenance, can run into the hundreds of thousands. This may be seen as dissipating an inheritance and cause conflict in fiduciary decision making.

For example, if your love is travel, today accessible travel, regardless of incapacity, is available to you, but the price of a skilled travel companion is high. Will a professional fiduciary/trustee spend the money and diminish the corpus of a trust for your benefit? Would they even know who could arrange travel for you safely, if you have a healthcare issue, such as heart or kidney ailments?

Only you, through documents and a portfolio poised for such expenditures, can make your golden years your best years.

We often read of wildly wealthy people, like Mrs. Astor, suffering in old age at the hands of their family fiduciaries.

How is this possible? It happens because great wealth is often very private and no one is privileged in the inner sanctum of the family to see the signs of abuse or decline.

Part of what our clients include in their advanced planning is wise gift-giving strategies. You will read about that in the next Chapter.

Helping the Giuliani Campaign

Chapter 25

Gifts and Trusts

When we make an investment decision for our clients, one of the many non-market issues we take into consideration is in whose name the portfolio is held?

In what type of entity is the portfolio held? It is likely that I will make a very different investment choice for a client if the asset is held in the name of an individual, rather than in the name of a trust for children. First, the law requires a high standard of prudence from a trustee. As an advisor, I want to help the trustee to obey that rule. Second, the goals or purpose of the investment dictates what is logical. Often the goal of a trust is very long-term management and tax savings, not short-term profit.

A trust is a written document by which one person or corporation, called a grantor, gives money to a second person or corporation, called a trustee, to hold for the benefit of a third person, called the beneficiary.

There are many variables in setting up a trust. For example, the income beneficiary (the one who gets the income earned by the trust fund as it goes along) and remainderman (the one who gets the trust fund itself when the trust terminates) can be the same person. The grantor (the person who transfers the money in the first place) can also be the trustee (the person who handles, invests, and distributes the money). The duration, purpose, and amount of money or type of assets placed in trusts can vary.

Trusts are governed by state law and states have different requirements for setting up trusts and different interpretations on the language of trusts. Theoretically, a trust with any type of grantor/trustee/beneficiary combination can be set up for any legal purpose.

For our purposes, the most significant feature of an irrevocable trust is that, properly created, a new taxpayer is born. The trust itself pays taxes to the government. Money earned by a trust fund is taxed to it, not to the grantor or to the beneficiary.

A trust files its own return if the grantor (the person setting up the trust) has little or no control over the use of the trust. Control is relinquished either by naming another person trustee or by giving oneself, as a trustee, limited powers over funds. Logic dictates. If the grantor can use the trust fund anyway he or she wishes, the government views the trust fund as merely a sham, a device to create a taxpayer in a lower tax bracket than the grantor.

Trust income may, instead, be taxed at the rate and bracket of the income beneficiary, if the beneficiary actually receives the income. If a trust fund earns interest, dividends, or increases in other ways and the trustee distributes this income or capital growth to the beneficiary, the beneficiary is taxed accordingly. If the trust accumulates the income or gain instead, the trust pays the tax.

What is the Prudent Person Rule?

If you are a fiduciary, please remember the Prudent Person Rule. Do not take risks with the money of minors. As a fiduciary, you are personally liable for losses as well as taxes. To be sure, you are liable for losses only if you could have foreseen them, and you were negligent in making the investment. So, you are not responsible if you made a perfectly natural or appropriate investment grade decision and took a loss. But, if you did take risks, such as putting money in commodity trading or highly speculative mutual funds, you could have personal liability.

A Quick Primer on Trusts.

InterVivos Trusts	Testamentary Trusts (in wills)
Saves on estate and income taxes	Controls use of money even after death
Allows you to see how your fiduciaries use and control your funds	Allow long range tax planning
Takes effect during your lifetime	Takes effect upon death
Gives away assets permanently if estate taxes are to be saved	Property remains yours during your lifetime
Can be revocable but then no estate taxes are saved	Property is taxed along with the rest of your estate
Can save on income taxes because they will be paid at either the trust's rate or the beneficiary's rate.	No income tax advantage

Professional Management

Trusts may help build wealth because they encourage professional management and continuity of management. By either naming a professional as trustee or using a professional to help build wealth, you are focusing and directing the professional to a special purpose.

Continuity

Another way that trusts build wealth is through the avoidance of intra-family squabbles. In some circumstances, you may wish to provide for one child and not another, or for your children in different degrees. At the end of your life, a will is made public to your beneficiaries and to your legal heirs. If legal heirs are discontent with their inheritance or lack thereof, they may contest the will. Even if they do not, many people are loath to disclose different treatment of their children. A trust is private. Its terms are known only by its grantor, trustee and beneficiary.

Perhaps even of greater practical importance is that the trust continues to be administered in the way you set forth during the period in which it may be attacked legally. By contrast, if a will is contested in probate the probate proceedings are prolonged, money remains in the estate without being managed, except by the executor during the contest, which may take many years. A trust, on the other hand, will continue to be administered, invested, and income distributed to the beneficiary of your choice even during the period of the contest.

If you are convinced that a trust is useful to you, your attorney is the proper professional to visit. If your attorney is an expert in estate planning, he or she will develop with you the kind of trust that you need to meet your goals. To prepare for your attorney's visit, we begin with the goal itself and take you through a checklist of needs on your personal horizon.

Probate Avoiding Trusts

Many use the revocable living trust to avoid probate. You may already be the trustee for your spouse (and vice versa), then a successor(s), usually an adult child or children are named. Single clients also usually name next of kin as trustees to take over at their death or if they become incompetent. All that is necessary is for the successor trustee to exercise the powers in the trust and there is no need for government intervention.

Right? Well, not quite. While there is no probate, the tax laws do apply in the same way as if there were a probate. When the grantor dies, the successor trustee must file an IRS form that requests a tax identification number, much like an individual's Social Security number.

Without it, the successor trustee cannot open accounts in the name of any of the testamentary trusts created by the terms of the revocable trust. Testamentary trusts are ones set up at death, such as minor's trusts, generation skipping trusts, charitable trusts or credit shelter marital trusts. In any case, they all need separate accounts, and that requires the tax identification number whether they are held in bank or brokerage institutions.

The successor trustee must also file the income tax form for trusts. If any income is immediately distributed by the trust to beneficiaries, the beneficiaries report the income on their tax returns. But, any retained income requires a reporting. The successor trustee MAY have to file form 706 with the IRS, the estate tax form.

This is where many people are misled. The 706 is the very same form that any estate must file to pay Federal estate taxes, whether the estate goes through traditional probate or not. There is no better or cheaper tax deal if there is a revocable trust instead of a will. Any taxes due must be paid within nine months, so the form must be filed within that period of time.

Trusts in a Will for the Children

Typically, you will leave your minor child's share with your surviving spouse as trustee. Similarly, you may create a trust for your grandchildren, naming their parents as trustees. Minors (under 18 or 21, depending on the state in which they live) cannot act as executors or trustees. With a substantial trust, a professional trustee is preferable.

If, instead of making an outright gift, you create a trust, you must decide whether to create one single trust for all your children or a separate trust for each child. The consequences of each method are largely tax-related and administrative. Both methods can distribute income to the children at the trustee's direction or provide for its accumulation. The trustee can invade the principal for educational purposes or for emergencies. You can specify separate trusts that will terminate, distributing the funds to each of your heirs at a different date. You can also terminate a single trust at a specific date and have the assets be distributed to each child at a different time.

Trusts for the Spendthrift

Spendthrift trusts are a protection against heirs spending trust income before it is distributed to them. Creditors such as jewelry stores and automobile salespeople were often willing to accept a note giving them the right to collect future trust-guaranteed income. The would-be heir often had all future income pledged to creditors. A spendthrift trust protects heirs and does not give them any interest in the income until it is distributed, so that they cannot give it away beforehand. Such trusts can also empower the trustee to make only direct payments for the needs of the beneficiary instead of giving them income.

Selecting the Trustee

Many parents wish to act as trustees for their children. By naming another as trustee, they may feel that they are relinquishing too much control over the money, and this may block actually setting up a trust. The last thing I want to accomplish is to put a chilling effect on any parent's desire to set up a trust by recommending that the only avenue is to select a professional trustee. It is certainly not necessary. I have managed the assets in dozens of trusts where the parents are the trustees. Yet, to be fair, it is my opinion that selecting a professional trustee is the best way.

Power Exercised by the Grantor

If you are the parent/grantor and also the trustee, and want to maintain some tax breaks, there are some powers that are strictly taboo for you to retain. If the grantor or any subordinates, such as a spouse, mother, father, sibling, child, employee, or corporation in which the grantor has a significant amount of stock, or an employee of such a corporation, has these powers, the grantor will have his tax bracket and rate applied to the income from the trust fund.

These strictly taboo powers should be specifically prohibited in the trust itself. In preparing a trust for a minor, most attorneys will do this automatically. The most significant of the taboos are:

1. The power to buy, exchange or deal with the trust income or principal for less than adequate consideration.

2. The power to borrow from the trust without adequate interest or security except when there is an independent trustee with the power to make loans.

3. The power to administer the trust in a non-fiduciary capacity without the consent of a fiduciary, such as the power to vote the stock of a corporation.

Any of these powers, and a handful of others, can cause the income to be taxed at the same bracket and rate as that of the grantor.

The grantor's rate and bracket will also be applied if the grantor can cause the income of the trust to be distributed to him or his spouse, or be held or accumulated for distribution to him or his spouse, or applied to the payment of premiums for insurance on his or her life or that of his or her spouse's life.

If the parent merely wishes to control when and whether the income or principal is paid to the child during the course of the trust for emergency needs, he or she can do so without any adverse tax consequences. That portion used for the child will be taxed to the parent. The parent might also wish to control the investments. This the parent cannot do, or else the entire trust would be tainted.

For example, if a parent is named trustee and his child has a health condition, under the terms of the trust, the parents can determine if the principal can be invaded in the event of a medical emergency and only that amount actually used for the child's health (an obligation of the parent himself under most state laws) will be taxed at the bracket/rate (B/R) of the parent.

If no medical emergencies arise and no use of principal is made, there will be no tax except at the trust B/R. On the other hand, if the trust allowed the parent to make investment decisions to the extent that property could be exchanged continually by the parent, the entire trust would be tainted; and it is likely that the B/R applied would be that of the parent, not the child.

What Is A Gift?

As we discuss it here, a gift is a transfer of property from your possession to the possession and ownership of another (in this case, your children). The key words are "actual transfer." Many parents believe that they can put a gift on an elastic string, giving it to the child and then snatching it back when they "need the money."

In fact, this is a very dangerous attitude. It can cause psychological problems if the child is old enough to be aware that a gift is being given and taken away. More usually, it can create legal problems since a true gift must be given with the intent to relinquish control. The government is interested in allowing you the various tax breaks that come with gift giving only when there are no elastic strings attached. Once a gift is given, it belongs to the person who receives the gift (the donee), not the person who gave the gift (the donor). Legal title has passed.

The most essential questions to consider in gift giving are:

- How much should I give?
- In what form shall I give it?
- What assets shall I give?

In answering these questions, use your instincts. Once given, a gift is out of your control. When we discuss the many ways of giving gifts, you will see that some dominion may continue; but for the most part, your power over the gifted funds is very limited. Remember, too, that gift giving, as we discuss it, is a financial and tax-saving device. Never trade your peace of mind for a tax advantage.

How Much Shall I Give?

The amount of your gift should be judged by tax considerations whenever possible. When a gift is given, a gift tax must be paid under certain circumstances. This seems odd to most people. Its purposes from the government's point of view are clear. The government presumes that the very purpose of giving the gift is to avoid the eventual estate taxes. In order to prevent people from divesting themselves of all their assets right before death, the government imposes gift taxes. This eliminates the incentive to give away all your property, or a substantial part of it, to save estate taxes.

Therefore, in giving gifts, it is wise to do so in a way that is gift tax free. Grandparents and other friends or relatives may give unlimited gifts to cover tuition or medical care costs without paying a gift tax. Caveat: such payments must be made directly to the school or health care institution. Parents cannot make such tax-free gifts because the exclusion does not apply to someone you have a legal obligation to support.

Outright Gifts

The simplest way of gift giving is to give the gift directly to the child. Many people do this without any policing by the government, the courts, or a fiduciary. If stamps, jewelry, or coins are given to children, there may have been a successful transfer, but there certainly is no guarantee that the money will be invested or used in any proper way. If cash, real estate, securities, bonds, or other assets are transferred to a minor, a minor can do little more than spend the money. In most states, a minor cannot create a trust, contract to hire a financial advisor, or even make a will. In some areas of the country, a minor cannot even rent a safe-deposit box.

Before a direct gift is made, the minor's fiscal responsibility should be considered. If anything does happen to the minor, the minor's estate will pay taxes on the amount. Most parents and grandparents would not dream of making actual transfers to minors without exercising any control over the gift. In fact, this is not always wise. In many states, age 21 is the age of majority. Yet there are also teenagers who have great fiscal responsibility and knowledge. The point is to consider each family member separately and try to avoid making a blanket decision for all of the children or grandchildren.

Legal Guardianship

Most grandparents feel that when they give their gift to a minor, it will be handled by the minor's parents. In the normal course of family life, this is probably so. There is, however, such a thing as a legal guardianship. The gift is given directly to the child, and yet there is an adult to guard the money and the child. These arrangements can be complicated, however, and you should consult with an attorney in structuring them.

Beneficial Ownership

In addition to outright ownership, there are several forms of beneficial ownership. Beneficial ownership allows a person or entity to enjoy all or some of the benefits of property ownership, except the right to dispose of legal ownership through deed or bequest.

Limited Present Interest

A limited present interest is a type of beneficial ownership given to a person or entity that becomes entitled to use, occupy, rent or enjoy the property for a specific period of time. That time can be for a given period of years, for a lifetime or for an unspecified time, ending with the happening of an event (such as marriage or emancipation of a minor). During the time that the limited interest is in effect, the beneficial owner may do everything that a legal owner may do except sell legal ownership. The beneficial owner can rent the property, live in the property and even sell his or her right to occupy.

Joint Ownership

Two kinds of gifts can be set up jointly: joint tenants and tenants in common. A joint tenancy creates ownership of the entire sum in both parties. Both you and the donee own the whole gift. Neither can sell nor otherwise transfer his or her share without the consent of the other. Neither may an owner use the property without the other's knowledge and consent. If you create a joint tenancy with your child and the child dies, the amount will be fully inherited by you, the surviving parent; if you die first, the amount is fully inherited by your child.

By contrast, with tenants in common each owns a half interest in the property. If one dies, his or her heirs, not the surviving half-owner, inherit.

Making Joint Gifts

We often create joint ownership between ourselves and a minor (our children and grandchildren). Many of us do this without realizing we are creating joint gifts. Here are a few examples:

1. A joint bank account opened in your name and a child's (or other's) name.

2. Purchasing a United States Bond in two names. The purchaser may cash in the bond tax-free; the other party would pay a gift tax upon cashing in the bond.

3. Purchasing joint stock. Naming a joint owner establishes that a gift has been made.

4. Putting real estate in another person's name. A gift is considered to have been made when the new deed is issued.

Custodial Bank Accounts: Be Aware of Potential Tax Problems

Many people open up an account in their own name together with a minor. For the most part, this is the creation of a joint account. There is confusion as to the proper method of taxing such an account. At least one tax court has held that interest earned on joint tenancies are taxable to the owners in proportion to their contribution.

Another court held that the contributions were immaterial, and the taxes were to be placed on an equal basis. Caution: An interesting point to consider is the use of Social Security numbers in opening up joint accounts. Frequently, a lower-tax-paying grandmother will, without informing her children or grandchildren, set up a joint account. The interest from that account is money that she expects to declare and pay taxes on at her lower B/R. If the Social Security number of the child is listed first, the IRS may consider the funds to be that of the child's.

What is the solution to the tax and control issues that comes with trusts and gifting? The answer is to create a team with your family, attorney and financial advisor working together and meeting regularly to achieve the result you desire.

Part VI: Coming to a Logical Conclusion

Chapter 26

Creating a Logical Path with Bite

There is a time-honored aphorism in the field of financial planning that goes like this, "People do not plan to fail. They fail to plan." Sometimes I wonder if people do not actively undermine themselves, and they do plan to fail!

Here is an example born of a conversation I had just three days before this writing. I was advising a 65-year-old client whom I consider one of the most brilliant men I have ever met. He built a two billion dollar business, in his words, "brick by brick." He began with a small manufacturing plant and created a privately owned mega business.

During the course of our conversation about money management, I got a truly major shock. I discovered he knew nothing about estate planning. He was fearful of giving control over to his children and had done no succession planning whatsoever. He was truly suffering from a natural fear of giving away 35 years of control.

A little bit of advanced planning would solve a big family and humongous tax issue. Without getting too detailed, he created a trust and moved non-voting shares of the company into the trust for the benefit of his children during his lifetime and with full ownership upon his death. In doing so, he had some leeway in valuation, which we would never have if the valuation came at date of death. In fact, the family might have been forced to sell the company to pay taxes.

It was important to do this while my client was still in his prime and might be running the company for the next 20 or 25 years. Why? The IRS has parameters for transferring value out of a company this large into a trust-like structure. He certainly could not have done any planning that would not have been scrutinized if he decided to take action six months before he sold, or if the family had its first planning session after his death.

Why do I relate this story?

I have thoroughly enjoyed writing this book, and I hope that you have gotten a great deal out of it from the point of view of some technical aspects of what we do, i.e., how we asset allocate and how we rebalance. But, none of that will make any difference if you fail to plan. What really stops a billion dollar genius from protecting his creation? It certainly was not greed. He had all the money he needed, and he knew it. Furthermore, the type of planning that he needed was about preservation, not growth.

No. Not greed, but fear.

You would be surprised how often even with the very successful, fear is a factor that interferes with logic. Fear of trusting others, fear of losing control, fear of getting old.

You know by now that I have asked you to dig deep, and determine what might be stopping you in your logical application of good planning when it comes to your money. One not so surprising factor is the cost. It is natural to wonder:

What Is Professional Money Management Going To Cost?

There is a definite cost to running a portfolio, and most people assume that it is much greater than it is. Most are also unaware of hidden costs in investing without a money manager. By comparison, true money management is actually less expensive than a do-it-yourself program. At least, ours can be. Once again, if you have more money to manage, the costs are proportionately less.

As I have written in earlier Chapters, there is a threshold below which it does not pay to have a money manager. Nevertheless, even going solo is going to cost you. With financial planning and investing, as in anything else in life, there is no free lunch. Just because no one is sending you a bill, does not mean you are not paying. For example, mutual funds, closed end funds and exchange traded funds all have internal costs.

Some of them are very difficult to understand, although all of them by law set forth costs in their prospectus. Even SPDRs, Standard and Poor's Depository Receipts, through which you can buy units in all of the S&P listed companies for the ultimate in unmanaged investing, costs 1/10 of 1%. Not much of a charge, but a charge, nevertheless. On the higher-end, highly-managed mutual funds may cost you up to 2 1/2% in internal management fees, PLUS commissions or "loads" on both ends, when you buy and when you sell.

What about your advisor or professional? They come in three varieties: 1) commission based, 2) fee based, 3) both.

If commission based, you will be charged transaction fees every time you buy or sell.

If fee based, you will be charged a management fee, usually billed quarterly. Or you may be charged a wrap fee - all transaction fees are included, but if a mutual fund is in your portfolio, the internal management fee for the fund will also be paid by you. Advisors, like RIAs, Registered Investment Advisors, are usually fee based.

At The Moldaver Group, we are fee based and do not charge trading fees. Our management fee is 1-1½% of the amount under management. Psychologically, we believe that this helps you, as you can see that we make more money on fees if there is more money under management. This means we have a pocketbook interest in increasing your portfolio. Sometimes the client will ask us simply to hold assets, like long-term bonds. We will surely do that, and not apply any fee whatsoever since we are not actively managing the holdings on any regular basis.

It is not logical to get hung up on fees

I know that may sound self-serving, but the fact remains that it is illogical to expect something for nothing.

I recall the commotion that took place over A and B shares of mutual funds. With A shares, the load/commission comes out upon purchase, so that less of your money is working for you.

With B shares, it comes out on a sliding scale; the yearly load disappears, if you hold the fund for five years or so, depending on the fund. B shares also charge 1% more in yearly management fees than A shares. Hundreds of articles and charts were published to show how much more money you would make with the B shares. Mathematically, of course, that's true if the fund loses money! If the fund makes money, you actually pay more with B shares.

What is more important to results than fees, is that you had a good money management team in the first place.

What about Unmanaged Accounts?

I chuckle when people tell me that they pay no commission on their bonds. It surely looks like that. They may not realize that the bond prices have been "marked up" from their original institutional price, to the financial advisor, and then marked up again by the financial advisor to the client. That markup might account for two years of gains in this low interest rate environment.

In our management accounts, we do not mark up our bonds. Only the management fee applies. If we hold an unmanaged bond portfolio for you for your convenience, we charge no fee.

I tell you this because one of the most illogical things you can do is believe you are saving money by not getting help.

As I have been writing this book, I have thought long and hard as to actually why our Moldaver Group was named as number one by Barron's. If truth be told, it is not exactly because we make more money for our clients than our competitors; although, our performance is stellar.

I believe it is something more fundamental than that. We create the results that our clients describe they want when we first set out their goals and objectives. Hitting the jackpot once in a while, or beating the market here and there, is not our claim to fame. Ours is bringing certainty into an increasingly uncertain world.

A Word about Ace

One of the people I admired the most and was a mentor of a kind to me was Alan "Ace" Greenberg. He began work at Bear Stearns in 1949 as a clerk. He served as Chairman of the Board of Bear Stearns from 1985 to 2001, and as its CEO from 1978 to 1993. He is and has been one of the biggest names on Wall Street. He sat down one-on-one with my clients and me on at least twenty-five to thirty different occasions. One of his most popular books was *Memos from the Chairman*.

One of the many things he taught me was simply to be available. Below you will see an actual memo he sent around. I carry it with me; the message is so important. It deals with people being available to clients and co-workers. One of the biggest gripes that clients have is that their advisors either do not return calls in a timely fashion or just are unavailable. That causes problems and could cause losses. That is why, in our Group, we are always reachable.

Memo

FROM THE DESK OF ALAN C. GREENBERG

To	All General & Limited Partners	Date	October 5, 1978
From	Alan C. Greenberg	CC	

Subject

    Bear Stearns is moving forward at an accelerated rate and everybody is contributing. It is absolutely essential for us to be able to talk to our partners at all times. All of us are entitled to eat lunch, play golf and go on vacation. But, you must leave word with your secretary or associates where you can be reached at all times. Decisions have to be made and your input can be important!

    I conducted a study of the 200 firms that have disappeared from Wall Street over the last few years, and I discovered that 62.349% went out of business because the important people did not leave word where they went when they left their desk if even for 10 minutes.

    That idiocy will not occur here.

Yes, I agree, "Ace," a financial advisor who is not available is unacceptable to me and should be to you, too.

This leads me to **The Bite Invite.**

Do not be a stranger. By all means, let us know if you would like a portfolio review. Please be kind enough to share this book with those you think are in need of financial logic. Contact me at ed.moldaver@stifel.com or emoldaver@gmail.com for personal or other matters.

As you might have noticed from our team bios, we are very charitably oriented. If you feel you have a charitable fundraising cause that would benefit from giving this book as a prize or even having one of our experts speak at an event, let us know. We offer support with full hearts and logical minds.

APPENDICES

Appendix I

The Oracle at Delphi Says: "Know Thyself"

Here come the data sheets! But, to paraphrase a line from "Alice in Wonderland": "When you do not know where you are going, any road will take you there."

Aimlessness is death to financial decision making. You must know what you own, how each asset is performing, what you need, and how well new investments do once you buy them. There is no other way to judge whether you are becoming a better decision maker. You will also need to set goals. It is hard to do that if you do not know how far away you are from your target.

But, I do not want the paperwork to get in your way or become an excuse for inaction. It is too easy to use the data sheets as a barrier to making a move - "I'll invest in stocks AFTER I get all the information on paper." "I have to call my accountant to get the information, and she's on vacation." "I'm terrible at math, so I'll wait until my husband (wife) has time to work with me." (It is nice to plan with your significant other; but, not as an excuse for procrastination.)

If there is any danger that the following paperwork will delay you from making an investment decision for more than two weeks, DO NOT DO IT! If you are a person that builds a wall between yourself and taking action with "make work" tasks, data gathering can be deadly.

Every minute your money works for you brings you closer to your independence. So, whether you are comfortable with data sheets or not, do not delay.

Now for the Data Gathering:

Take stock of your goals. Have your significant other do the same. Make special note (but do not discuss, as yet) areas, if any, where your goals are in conflict.

Financial Goals and Objectives

On a scale from 0 to 5, circle the number to the right of each of the items below that most accurately reflects your financial concerns. A 5 would signify a priority item, and a 0 would indicate that the particular topic has no impact on this planning process.

A. Current Financial Situation—Do You Wish to...

Improve your present standard of living	1 2 3 4 5
Increase your net worth	1 2 3 4 5
Increase available disposable income	1 2 3 4 5
Provide a hedge against inflation	1 2 3 4 5
Provide funds for a capital expenditure	1 2 3 4 5

B. If you have young children, will you...

Accumulate college tuition	1 2 3 4 5
Provide only a portion of tuition	1 2 3 4 5
Seek financial aid	1 2 3 4 5

C. How important is tax reduction/deferral? 1 2 3 4 5

D. Which describes your portfolio preferences

    Liquidity 1 2 3 4 5

    Safety of principal 1 2 3 4 5

    Present income 1 2 3 4 5

    Long term growth 1 2 3 4 5

    Tax Benefits 1 2 3 4 5

E. I would like to invest in my own business 1 2 3 4 5

F. Retirement income: Do you wish to...

    Maintain you standard of living 1 2 3 4 5

    Change your lifestyle (e.g., more travel) 1 2 3 4 5

    Sell existing assets to fund retirement 1 2 3 4 5

G. For your dependents, do you wish to...

    Provide guaranteed income on your death 1 2 3 4 5

Provide guaranteed income if disabled	1 2 3 4 5
Preserve assets if disabled	1 2 3 4 5

H. Charity—would you like to provide...

Charitable bequest on your death	1 2 3 4 5
Charitable gifts now	1 2 3 4 5

I. Rank these in terms of importance

Current income	1 2 3 4 5
Investments	1 2 3 4 5
Educational fund	1 2 3 4 5
Retirement	1 2 3 4 5
Taxes	1 2 3 4 5
Asset protection	1 2 3 4 5
Charity	1 2 3 4 5

> Make sure you also have your financial co-decision makers fill out these materials, as well.

Excerpted and paraphrased from Adriane G. Berg's "Your Wealthbuilding Years" (Newmarket Press, 1994).

Net Worth Statement

		WHEN	COST	PURCHASE PRICE	PRESENT MARKET VALUE	TAX STATUS	% OF PORTFOLIO	CURRENT VALUE	M Ye G
CASH & EQUIVALENT									
	CASH & SAVINGS								
	CHECKING								
	CASH VALUE OF INSURANCE								
	METALS								
INCOME GENERATORS									
	CDs								
	CMOs								
	BOND FUNDS								
	TAX FREE FUNDS								
	TAX FREE BONDS								
	MUNICIPAL BONDS								
	UNIT TRUSTS								
	TREASURIES								
	ZERO COUPON BONDS								
	FIXED ANNUITIES								
	CORPORATE BONDS								
	FOREIGN BONDS								
	MORTGAGE								

NET WORTH STATEMENT

TOTALS

CASH   _____

INCOME GENERATORS   _____

EQUITIES   _____

SPECULATIONS   _____

                    TOTAL ASSETS   _____

Liabilities

	Amount Owed	Late Charges	Due Date	Interest Rate	Collateral	Payment Period (monthly)
Mortgage #1						
Mortgage #2						
Home Equity Loan						
College Loan						
Car Loans						
Personal Loan #1						
Personal Loan #2						
Credit Card #1						
Credit Card #2						

QUICK INCOME AND EXPENSE STATEMENT

From _____ 20____ to _____
                     20____
(to cover one year)

INCOME Money you receive.

GROSS SALARY/WAGES $_____

    MINUS DEDUCTIONS
    Federal and State income tax, FICA, etc. $_____

        TAKE-HOME PAY $_____

OTHER GROSS SALARY/WAGES
IN HOUSEHOLD $_____

MINUS DEDUCTIONS $_____

    TAKE-HOME PAY $_____

COMMISSIONS, TIPS, BONUSES $_____

NET PROFIT FROM BUSINESS,
FARM, TRADE, PROFESSION $_____

INTEREST OR DIVIDENDS FROM
SAVINGS, STOCKS, BONDS, OTHER
SECURITIES, NOTES $_____

NET PROFIT FROM SALES OF ASSETS $_____

NET PROFIT FROM RENTAL PROPERTY $_____

INCOME FROM ALIMONY/CHILD SUPPORT $_____

REFUNDS/REBATES $_____

CASH GIFTS $_____

OTHER INCOME
    Social Security Benefits $_____

    Individual Retirement Accounts, Keoghs $_____

    Pensions, annuities $_____

Veterans benefits	$_____
Unemployment benefits	$_____
Disability benefits	$_____
Life Insurance benefits	$_____
Income from trusts	$_____
Royalties/residuals	$_____

TOTAL INCOME

$_____

EXPENSES Money you spend, including self-established savings goals/

RENT Include utility payments if automatically included in rent. $_____

MORTGAGE PAYMENTS Include property tax and insurance if automatically included in payment. $_____

OTHER REAL ESTATE Second mortgage, home improvement loan (if secured by home), vacation home, storage rental, homeowners' association fees. $_____

HOUSEHOLD MAINTENANCE/REPAIR
Gardening, cleaning house/appliance repairs (materials, labor). $_____

UTILITIES Gas, electricity, heating, fuel, phone, water, cable TV, garbage. $_____

FOOD Groceries, nonfood items in supermarket bill. $_____

TRANSPORTATION Car operating expenses (gas, repairs, servicing), parking, public transportation. $_____

CREDIT/CHARGE ACCOUNTS Payments for charge accounts, credit cards, personal lines of credit. $_____

INSTALLMENT CONTRACT PAYMENTS
Payments made a regular intervals over specific time periods for purchase of vehicle, mobile home, furniture and so on. $_____

Appendix II

Trust Glossary

Excerpted from "Moneythink," by Adriane Berg, Pilgrim Press:

Trust. A written document whose purpose is to put your money in the hands of a third party, so that the third party can use it only for the benefit of your loved one.

Trustee. The person to whom you entrust oversight, so that he or she can handle assets for your loved one.

Beneficiary. The loved one, the person you wish to get the benefit of the trust.

Corpus. This is Latin for "body," but here it means the money itself or the bonds, stocks, diamonds, or whatever else you wish to give to the trustee for the benefit of the beneficiary.

Settlor or grantor. The person who creates the trust.

Revocable trust. A trust that the settlor can revoke at will.

Irrevocable trust. A trust that the settlor cannot terminate; it goes on without control by the settlor once it has been made.

Inter vivos trusts. The Latin literally means "between" (inter) and "living persons" (vivos). These are trusts that you create during your lifetime. You can even be the trustee settlor). The trust can terminate on your death or during your own lifetime. One that you create during your lifetime can pour over into another trust in your will so that it continues even after your death.

Testamentary trusts. These trusts are created only in your will and come into action only upon your death. They are part of your last will and testament. If you change your will, you can eliminate them. Of course, if you already have an inter vivos trust, you can instruct in your will what to do with it. This is called a "pour-over" provision if your instructions are to take inter vivos trust funds and "pour" them into a testamentary (set up by will) trust fund.

Appendix III

Logic-A Very Short Course

Here is an academic definition of logic—you will see that it is not about formula but about reasoning:

The term "logic" came from the Greek word *logos*, which is sometimes translated as "sentence," "discourse," "reason," "rule," and "ratio." Of course, these translations are not enough to help us understand the more specialized meaning of "logic" as it is used today.

So what is logic? Briefly speaking, we might define logic as *the study of the principles of correct reasoning*. Source: http://philosophy.hku.hk

When it comes to investing, logic is separate from emotions or psychology; but in practice, it is usually your emotions that prevent you from applying logic.

Here is another quote from http://philosophy.hku.hk:

"One thing you should note about this definition is that logic is concerned with the principles of *correct* reasoning. Studying the correct principles of reasoning is not the same as studying the *psychology* of reasoning. Logic is the former discipline, and it tells us how we *ought* to reason if we want to reason correctly.

Whether people actually follow these rules of correct reasoning is an empirical matter, something that is not the concern of logic.

The psychology of reasoning, on the other hand, is an empirical science. It tells us about the actual reasoning habits of people, including their mistakes. A psychologist studying reasoning might be interested in how people's ability to reason varies with age. But such empirical facts are of no concern to the logician.

So what are these principles of reasoning that are part of logic? There are many such principles, but the main (not the only) thing that we study in logic are *principles governing the validity of arguments*—whether certain conclusions follow from some given assumptions."

Now I hope you can see why I rely so heavily on logic to create and protect my clients' wealth. I cannot predict the future. But, I can extrapolate from my knowledge to make assumptions and then reason as to whether certain conclusions follow from those assumptions.

Let us look at the way this works, first from an example from the online course I mentioned. I found it ironic that their example was about money. Then I will use the same reasoning with an example about logical investing.

Here is their example of applied logic:

>If Tom is a philosopher, then Tom is poor.
>Tom is a philosopher.
>Therefore, Tom is poor.
>If $K>10$, then $K>2$.
>$K>10$
>Therefore, $K>2$.

If Tarragona is in Europe, then Tarragona is not in China.
>Tarragona is in Europe.
>Therefore, Tarragona is not in China.

These two arguments are obviously good arguments in the sense that their conclusions follow from the assumptions. If the assumptions of the argument are true, the conclusion of the argument must also be true. A logician will tell us that they are all cases of a particular form of argument known as "*modus ponens*."

Now, let us look at three examples of applied logic directly from the world of investing, and you will see the three main functions of a financial advisor:

When inflation increases, the cost of many goods and services goes up.
Inflation is increasing.
The cost of many goods and services will go up.

When interest rates fall, bond prices rise.
Interest rates are falling.
Bond prices will rise.

Insurance pays the beneficiary family death benefits when the insured dies.
All people die.
All insured beneficiary families will receive death benefits.

So here we see the three areas where logic and investment Bite meet.

> #1. Knowledge: In the first example, the advisor needs to know the validity of the assumption that inflation and cost of living (goods and services) have a relationship and what relationship that is. The same applies to interest rates and bond values. So here the advisor exercises logic to make an investment conclusion and acts dispassionately.
>
> #2. Experience for detecting faulty assumptions or aberrant markets: The fact is that not all philosophers are poor, as in the course's example. Actually, Socrates, Aristotle, and Plato were rich guys. But many are poor. Sometimes interest rates go down, not up, and so do bond prices. Advisors need to apply

different conclusions when they detect that the usual assumptions do not apply. They detect these aberrations through years of experience.

#3. Dispassion: In the third example, the advisor accepts the inevitable and makes sure the client is insured, without the resistance to our own mortality that we all share.

Logic is topic-neutral: Before we leave this very brief dissertation on philosophy and logic, let us look at something called "topic-neutrality" and how it applies to the function of financial planning, which includes, but is bigger than investing.
According to our course in philosophy, logic is topic-neutral. Its principles apply in all disciplines.
Modus ponens might be used to illustrate the feature of logic's topic-neutrality. As the examples suggest, *modus ponens* can be used in reasoning about diverse topics. This is true of all the principles of reasoning in logic. The laws of biology might be true only of living creatures, and the laws of economics are only applicable to collections of agents that engage in financial transactions. But, the principles of logic are universal principles which are more general than biology and economics.

Appendix IV

What Billionaires Know

Oddly enough, one of the most important traits of the billionaire that they do share is their respect for small amounts of money and incremental returns. If you invest $1 million over 10 years and can earn an extra 1%, that will make a difference of $259,000.

1% DIFFERENCE IN ANNUAL RATE COMPOUNDED OVER 10 YEARS

YEAR	ANNUAL 8%	RATE OF 9%	RETURN 10%
1	$ 1,000,000	$ 1,000,000	$ 1,000,000
2	$ 1,080,000	$ 1,090,000	$ 1,100,000
3	$ 1,166,400	$ 1,188,100	$ 1,210,000
4	$ 1,259,712	$ 1,295,029	$ 1,331,000
5	$ 1,360,489	$ 1,411,582	$ 1,464,100
6	$ 1,469,328	$ 1,538,624	$ 1,610,510
7	$ 1,586,874	$ 1,677,100	$ 1,771,561
8	$ 1,713,824	$ 1,828,039	$ 1,948,717
9	$ 1,850,930	$ 1,992,563	$ 2,143,589
10	$ 1,999,005	$ 2,171,893	$ 2,357,948

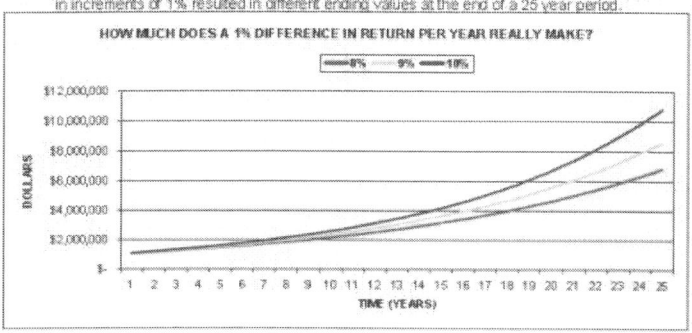

All three portfolios began with an initial investment of $1,000,000. Different annual rates of return in increments of 1% resulted in different ending values at the end of a 25 year period.

HOW MUCH DOES A 1% DIFFERENCE IN RETURN PER YEAR REALLY MAKE?

Billionaires take calculated risks.

Billionaires take risks often looking for three times better than index performance over the long haul, usually five to ten years. Lesser performing investors are looking for a quick fix.

Billionaires go for Bite.

Billionaires also know that there is a right way and a wrong way to manage money. They shun over speculation. They shun The Fluff in favor of The Bite. They do not buy or sell on hype.

Billionaires do not buy the story

One of my favorite Fluff stories is the story of the BlackBerry cell phone. Everyone needed to own it. It was the next big thing. It was all over our social media. The whole shebang went down about 90% in the ultimate lackluster company performance.

Nine times out of ten the story does not deliver. But we do tend to buy the story. It is just so tempting. Perhaps I can tell you how I discipline myself to avoid falling for The Fluff.

No, it is not an emotional discipline, it is a mathematical discipline. I avoid what is called "momentum stocks." Those are stocks that are growing in price exponentially. If the stock usually grows at 1% a month and instead grows 2% in the second month 4% in the third, 5% in the fifth month etc. it has momentum. Usually, that means it has a story. If it did not have some media hype, investors would be buying more slowly, more judiciously; fund managers would be waiting for quarterly reports. But, when you see momentum, you know there is some story behind that momentum.

Now, of course, a momentum stock could be a long-lasting outperformer of the market. So, I do not stop there. Now, I see whether or not this is also a value stock. Again, I use the numbers. I look at the internal rate of return of that company to investors over the past ten years. I look to see if the price of the stock is less than the value of the company. Simple mathematics, if there are 100 shares of stock issued, and the company would sell for $1,000, each share should sell for $10. If shares are currently selling for $9.50, that is a value stock. I must admit that I rarely have found a momentum stock to also be a value stock. But, it happens.

And, that is still not all I do when there is a big story. I next go to the best managers that follow that industry or even that company. I want the guy who is glued to that industry and who has the good advisory team around him to catch what I may have missed. I am not looking for the advisors that deal with ETF's or generalists.

Getting it right is tricky. Even in the darkest stages of 2008, the market still had the appearance of a growth stage, up until virtually the last minute. Fortune Magazine's most admired companies in 2007 included Bear Stearns. Bear Stearns had the best years of their history, and they went bust.

A great majority crashed in excess of what they thought would happen. When things are trading as low as they have been in years, ask yourself is this permanent or temporary? And what do we mean by permanent? Can we expect to see this continue over the next six months or will prices achieve equilibrium more quickly?

How do we know the answer to this? We would look at industry articles to see if production costs are the problem, if raw material costs are the problem or there is lessening demand or more competition from other companies.

When we can identify the reason for a fall in any one industry or in the overall market, we can pretty well gauge what is needed to fix the problem. Then we take the next step. Who needs to fix the problem? Is it the FED? Is it company leadership? Is it a world power crisis?

And then we assess the risk of the fix not taking place. We do all of these steps with the help of the leading analysts in the field. There is no Bark or Fluff. Just The Bite.

Still that is not all there is to it. If we detect that a correction might not come soon, but the fundamentals of the company is good, that is the time we would be buying more. That is the way a decision with Bite makes sure money; it teaches you how to buy low.

I am a book collector. But, my collection is probably boring to most. I enjoy collecting all books on investing. I get a kick out of one of my favorite books which is simply 1,000 pages of stocks that do not exist today.

Every one of the companies failed. I look at it to remind me of an important axiom in logical investing. "Do not ever fall in love with a stock." You would be shocked at how many smart people have loyalty to a company because it was their first stock, or because they worked in the company, or because they think a deceased loved one had loyalty to the company.

Throughout this book, I quote words of wisdom from a book written in 1906, which teaches the same lessons we should all learn today.

In essence, all individual investing is a matter of behavioral psychology.

Made in the USA
Middletown, DE
02 May 2016